SEX ACTS

SEX ACTS

Practices of Femininity and Masculinity

Jennifer Harding

SAGE Publications
London • Thousand Oaks • New Delhi

First published 1998

SAGE Publications Ltd
6 Bonhill Street
London EC2A 4PU

SAGE Publications Inc
2455 Teller Road
Thousand Oaks, California 91320

SAGE Publications India Pvt Ltd
32, M-Block Market
Greater Kailash – I
New Delhi 110 048

British Library Cataloguing in Publication data

A catalogue record for this book is
available from the British Library

ISBN 0 8039 7594 5
ISBN 0 8039 7595 3 (pbk)

Library of Congress catalog card number 98–61235

Typeset by M Rules
Printed in Great Britain by Redwood Books, Trowbridge, Wiltshire

CONTENTS

ACKNOWLEDGEMENTS

I thank all those who have supported and encouraged my academic work over the last eight years. I am very grateful to friends and colleagues at the University of Technology Sydney, especially Marsha Rosengarten, Jeannie Martin, Norie Neumark and my colleagues in the Communications Department at London Guildhall University. Deidre Pribram's friendship and wit has been inspirational and Sharon Laura has been a great support. I thank my parents for always believing in me. I thank Fiona and Gabriel for fun, love and joyful distractions. This book is for them.

1

THE POWER OF SEX –
AN INTRODUCTION

Sex and society

Sexuality today is highly 'plastic'.[1] It represents a huge field of potential desires and is invested with many different meanings. Sexuality is the object of intense cultural fascination. It is also highly contested. Its contestability opens the way for numerous strategies aimed at defining and regulating what 'the sexual' comprises. Indeed, sexuality is a major focus of interest in academia, politics and popular culture where it is subject to attempts to define, explain and change it.

Sexuality has been a focal point for political activism throughout the nineteenth and twentieth centuries. Sexuality is the object over and through which control and liberation have been sought in conservative and radical campaigns for 'social purity', eugenics, sex reform, sexual liberation, access to birth control and abortion. Sexual agendas also intersect with other political agendas. For example, sexuality is at the centre of gender, race and class politics in local and global campaigns against forced sterilisations of poor and black women, pornography, paedophile rings and sex tourism. Sexuality has been extensively researched from a variety of theoretical and political perspectives, including biomedical, historical, anthropological, psychoanalytic, psychological, sociological, literary theory, feminist and lesbian and gay studies. Most recently, sexuality has been interrogated as part of a growth in analyses of the body and theorisation of the bodily roots of subjectivity. Lesbian and gay sexualities, currently more visible in the media and popular culture, are increasingly represented as exciting, fashionable and glamorous (Hamer and Budge, 1994).

One cumulative effect of the many attempts to represent and explain 'the sexual' has been to foreground sexuality as an extremely powerful force in (post)modern societies. This is based, in part, on the perceptions that sexuality is a crucial ingredient in the constitution of the subject and point of connection between the individual and social body, whereby the individual is integrated into the social order through the regulation and control of sexuality. In this sense, sexuality has been viewed as a private matter, an expression of the essential and intimate nature of the individual, which has broader consequences for 'society'.

Most commentators insist that an enormous degree of power infuses sexuality, yet work with different concepts of power. Different theoretical/political approaches entail different views of what sexuality is and how and why it is significant for individuals and societies. These variations demonstrate that sex is not a universal or consistent category of experience, but one that is culturally and historically constituted (Weeks, 1989).

In the 1990s, sexual possibilities appear infinite and the volume of theoretical and political writing about sexuality is rapidly expanding. What is so interesting, indeed fascinating, about sexuality? How much, after all, can be done and named as sexuality? Why add another book to the pile? Firstly, I think, there is a need to reflect critically on how and why sexuality has become an object of academic interrogation and what if anything can be learned and taught about/through it. Secondly, and most importantly, the existing literature has opened up some avenues of critical significance which warrant further investigation. *Sex Acts* critically examines some aspects of contemporary discourse on sexuality and analyses some hitherto unexplored elements of sexuality.

Points of departure

Since the 1970s, feminist, lesbian and gay researchers/activists have played a key role in emphasising the 'constructed' nature of sexuality and gender identity, and, importantly, have argued that the personal and seemingly private experience of sex is also political, historical and public. However, much of this work has not fully investigated the relation between sex and sexuality and the constitution of the sexed body. Many take as given an already existing (though differently interpreted and inscribed) sexed body and treat the categories 'private' and 'public' as unproblematically discrete.

To some extent, Michel Foucault's interrogation of sexuality and its relation to the category 'sex' in *The History of Sexuality* (1981) has opened up some of this ground, although Foucault's argument is (some would say) highly abstract, 'gender blind' and, possibly, over-emphasises the significance of discourse. Judith Butler's critical analysis of the work of key contemporary theorists effectively unseats the idea of *fixed* gendered identities grounded in nature, bodies or heterosexuality (Butler, 1990a).[2] In *Gender Trouble*, Butler effectively deconstructs heterosexuality and upsets the logic which maintains it as a dominant, obligatory, 'compulsory' sexuality in contemporary societies. She contests the idea that a naturally occurring *a priori* sex is expressed through a gender and then through a sexuality – heterosexuality – and develops a 'performative theory of gender', in which gender identity is not an attribute of an individual, but an act which must be repeatedly performed.

Butler's idea that gender performances are all parody and imitation has a great deal going for it. However, she is sparing with her empirical examples and her theoretical arguments are not easily accessible. Historically, the notion of performance fits more closely with popular cultural perceptions that femininity is an elusive ideal which must be constantly sought but never attained, and with some feminist descriptions of femininity as an identity in process, never complete. How then do the concepts 'gender performance' and 'parody' work for subjects (allegedly) pulled together by the sign 'men'? Also, if sex must be continually enacted and reinvented, performances are neither arbitrary nor entirely elective. As Butler's text indicates, there is much empirical work to be done to ascertain how cultural, historical and political factors compel and constrain enactments of sexed identity and how sexed meanings are/may be contested. Which specific constraints operate on and produce the sexed body as an anchor for significations of gender and 'the sexual' (Butler, 1990a)? How, as Butler asks, might the body be (re)signified beyond a binary frame? In an attempt to address these questions, this book includes a series of essays on performances of sex/uality, or, practices of femininity and masculinity.

The increased visibility of 'disavowed' sexualities in mainstream media, academia and politics raises some further interesting questions about identity and essentialism and definitions of 'the public' and 'the private'. Sexuality is persistently in the public eye, publicly dissected and judged, yet it maintains the appearance of an exquisitely private domain. The border separating the public/private appears exceedingly fragile but highly significant, as is revealed through the political acts of 'coming out' and 'outing' public figures (whether closet homosexuals or adulterous heterosexuals). The durability of the dichotomies private/public and inside/outside and their intersections is puzzling since no one is ever entirely either 'in' or 'out' of public view. Both elements of each pair are deeply implicated in, and exert some pressure on, the other. Even a 'romanticisation of the outside as a privileged site of radicality' is misplaced since, according to Diana Fuss, to idealise the outside one must to some extent already be 'comfortably entrenched on the inside' (Fuss, 1991). This line of inquiry leads again to questions about identity. The tensions between private and public domains as they operate through sex/uality are myriad, complex and important, and deserve further investigation.

Sex Acts challenges the assumption that sex is natural, intractable and self-evidently written on the body. It investigates relations between sex and sexuality and the tensions permeating the private/public aspects of sex/uality. This book explores ambiguities and the borders supporting sexual identities by analysing specific practices of femininity and masculinity at an empirical, ordinary and everyday level without taking any of these categories for granted. It sets these critical inquiries against a background of key discourses on sexuality and offers a critical handle on these.

The main foci of *Sex Acts* are: (1) an exploration of how sexuality straddles public and private domains and the implications of this; (2) an investigation of specific performances of sex/uality and practices of femininity and masculinity through a series of empirical case studies.

Sex Acts has grown out of doctoral research which I conducted at the University of Technology Sydney and my current research and under-graduate teaching at London Guildhall University. Overall, the book reflects my desire to bring some challenging theories to bear on everyday empirical circumstances to see what happens, and, hopefully, to open up some new political ground.

In *Sex Acts* I develop my earlier analyses of the construction of the cate-gories 'women' and 'the female body' in medical and feminist discourse (Harding, J., 1993, 1996, 1997) and the representation of lesbians in popular culture (Harding, J., 1994). I also examine the production of male bodies, masculinity and heterosexuality. This is based on the logic that a focus on those 'marginalised' by current structures of power may leave the 'centre' undeconstructed and fail to shift prevailing power relations (Fuss, 1991). This logic provokes the problematisation of what is taken to be 'at the centre' and the historicisation of the signifying practices through which identity categories are produced. However, margins and centres are not homoge-neous spaces, nor clearly demarcated one from the other. Being employed within the academy makes it hard to speak from and for the margins and to critique the centre as if you were apart from it. Academic knowledges are consistently founded on the space of alterity (Clifford, 1986; Losche, 1989/90). My selection of empirical case studies is influenced by these con-cerns, and by my recent experience of pregnancy and motherhood.

The next three chapters set the theoretical/political scene for my think-ing about sex/uality. The theoretical themes and conceptual tools elaborated in these chapters are developed throughout the rest of the book, which comprises a series of essays on performances of sex/uality (or, prac-tices of masculinity and femininity) and considers how the meanings of sex/uality are compelled, constrained and contested through these.

I take up and develop Michel Foucault's concepts of power and dis-course – in particular, the ideas that, firstly, discourses are not superstructures but practices that are lived, acted out and spoken by individuals and oper-ate as fields of fluid and mobile relations which produce power/ knowledge and, secondly, power is positive, productive and creative (Foucault, 1981, 1986). I also take up and develop Stuart Hall's and Judith Butler's rethinking of cultural politics and the processes of representation (Hall, 1990, 1992; Butler, 1990a, 1992a) – in particular, the ideas that subjects and identities do not pre-exist political endeavours to represent them but must be made and remade, in history and discourse. The task of poli-tics/theory is to investigate the process of constructing the subject and its political meanings in specific (political/theoretical) discourse. Identities are invented through attempts to represent them and are always incomplete and always in process (Hall, 1990). This is the case in all representations, whether part of conservative or radical projects.

Several key arguments are developed throughout this book. Firstly, the argument that discourses transmit, and are indistinguishable from, knowledge and power relations (Foucault, 1979, 1986). Following on from this, the second argument asserts that subjects of discourse are constructed within power relations (Foucault, 1986), which also constitute the horizons in which individuals act as an integral part of their capacities to act (Butler, 1992a: 10).[3] Thirdly, since power relations do not stop producing the effects of power, the construction of the subject is never complete, and subjectivity must be repeatedly 'resignified' (Butler, 1992a: 13). *All* discourses (including those designated 'dominant' and 'alternative' or 'reverse') bring into being and characterise the subjects for whom and to whom they speak, and delimit the capacities and horizons in terms of which they may act. I concentrate on the effects of power and the construction of subjectivity as they become apparent at the level of discourse.

In Chapter 2 I discuss previous approaches to studying sex. I do not present an exhaustive review of this area of inquiry, since this has been done by others;[4] rather, I highlight core aspects of the field in order to situate and develop my empirical studies. I examine debates about 'essentialism' and 'constructionism' in sex research, contrasting essentialist and constructionist assumptions about how 'the sexual' is constituted. I investigate the implications of the essentialist view that sexuality is a 'natural' phenomenon, outside of culture and society, comprising fixed and inherent drives, which determine sexual identities. I look at the ways in which 'sexologists' have attempted to bring sexuality under the control of science. I investigate constructionist arguments that sexuality has no inherent essence but must be understood as culturally and historically constituted within power relations. This line of investigation also involves consideration of the constructive, creative and gendered character of scientific activity in contrast to the prevailing belief (amongst sexologists/scientists) that science is objective and impartial. 'Nature' is examined as a powerful and variable historical *construct*. In response to essentialist/constructionist debate, I elaborate my approach to studying sex based on understanding sexuality *as* discourse and analysing discourse, based on Foucault's concept of discourse.

Chapter 3 examines the (ambiguous) relation of sexuality to the historical constitution of 'the private' and 'the public' as separate spheres and the political effects of transgressing the border dividing them. It looks at some of the legacies of the nineteenth century. These include the constitution of sexuality as 'symbolic' of wider social features, the concomitant deflection of major disruptions onto the sphere of sexuality, and the gendering of this process and the differentiation of public and private spheres. This chapter also examines the role of science as a 'sexualising' discourse which produces the ideas of sex it is claimed to describe and naturalises them. It discusses technologies of visualisations and the various ways in which power, since the Enlightenment, has been coupled with vision. The significance of Foucault's concept of *bio-power* is then considered in relation to contemporary public health discourse on risk and sexual health.

In Chapter 4 I discuss the role of the media in defining 'the sexual' and constituting the private and the public as distinctive spaces. I look at how acts of 'coming out' are manufactured and orchestrated by various media of mass communication and consider the significance of this, particularly for lesbians and gays. I examine concepts of 'identity' and ideas about how representation works. I take up Hall's argument that representation is a constructive act, which constitutes the phenomena which it appears to describe. That is, the media are not vehicles for meanings and identities which already exist but a process through which they are produced and invented (Hall, 1990). I discuss concepts of sex and gender (including the sex/gender debate) and their relation to sexuality, focusing on the work of Foucault and Butler. I discuss Butler's theory of gender performance, based on the idea that gender is an act rather than an attribute – a *doing*, rather than a *being*. I put forward a rationale for writing sex/uality.

Chapters 5 and 6 are concerned with discourses (scientific, feminist and popular cultural) on sex hormones which construct and contest a hormonally controlled body, and make sex hormones the cause of sex-gender-sexuality. In Chapter 5 I examine the early history of sex hormone research and the apparent 'power of hormones' as major twentieth-century inventions. I examine the emergence of the construct *the hormonal body* (meaning *the body controlled by hormones*) as a political way of conceptualising the body and the biological basis of sexual difference in all its manifestations. I argue that hormonal explanations of behaviour and feelings are brought into play as corrective or normalising strategies, which depoliticise events. The development of technologies to measure and adjust hormones has meant that deviant characteristics and behaviours can be 'corrected' at the level of the body, precluding a political account of events in favour of a biological explanation. Historically, the scientific study of sex hormones has been linked with efforts to manage and treat deviant sex/uality, typically problematised in women as being the result of unbalanced hormonal impulses and drives. This chapter specifically examines biomedical and feminist discourses on hormone replacement therapy (HRT) in relation to the idea of gender performance, looking at the ways in which they regulate and restrict performances of gender. It discusses the versions of ageing female sexuality produced through these discourses and highlights their differences and similarities. I argue that both biomedical and feminist discourses tend to produce the idea of 'natural' (and, therefore, immutable) sex as the foundation of various (albeit contested) manifestations of gender.

In Chapter 6 I examine recently publicised concerns about the adverse effects on the male body of 'environmental oestrogens' which, it is claimed, are 'feminising' men. I explore the implications of these concerns for practices of masculinity and for theorising gendered embodiment and identity. Here, I am interested in how and when men become variously embodied and the body is constituted as male. I explore some local sites where the male heterosexual body is organised and represented – that is, produced and invented – through selected media texts. This constitutes an attempt to deconstruct aspects of 'the centre', instead of focusing solely on groups marginalised by existing power relations. In both Chapters 5 and 6 I argue that biomedical discourse on sex hormones constitutes a very pervasive and powerful account of sex/uality, which delimits and constrains possible enactments of sex.

In Chapters 7 and 8 I examine motherhood and fatherhood (to a lesser degree) as highly variable gendered performances. In Chapter 7 I consider the ways in which contemporary (postmodern) reproductive bodies are constituted as cyborgs which, with the help of specific new reproductive technologies, makes possible a disassociation of sex-gender-sexuality and redesigning of the traditional family. I discuss the *medicalisation* of the maternal body and the limits of the 'medicalisation critique' in feminist discourse. I examine possible distinctions between modern and postmodern approaches to reproduction, in which postmodern approaches emphasise consumer choice, difference and customisation (Clarke, 1995). I focus on the political issues raised by recent proposals to address the shortage of donated ova by using tissue obtained from cadavers and aborted foetuses, and consider the ways in which motherhood is compelled as a gendered performance as well as the vexed (historical) feminist focus on 'choice'.

Chapters 8 and 9 highlight diversity 'on the margins'. In Chapter 8, as elsewhere I examine the various ways in which possible re-creations of the heterosexual nuclear family are resisted. I look at examples of queer (that is, non-traditional heterosexual married) family units, focusing on lesbian mothers, single teenage mothers and teenage fathers, and the ways in which these have been (re)presented as problematic sex/ualities in recent media texts. I show that these productions of troublesome sexualities are constituted in relation to 'choice' and, as its necessary precondition, economic independence. This chapter opens up a space for considering 'class' in relation to sexuality. This theme is continued in Chapter 9, which examines the representation of lesbians in popular culture as an attempt at securing the ontological boundaries of heterosexuality, and retraces the main themes of the book as a whole. It illustrates the pervasiveness and persuasiveness of 'compulsory heterosexuality' and discourses producing it as well as the fragility and contingencies of heterosexuality and gender identity. It demonstrates that sex/uality constitutes, above all, a site of intense contestation.

Notes

1.   Anthony Giddens uses the term 'plastic sexuality' to mean 'decentred sexuality, freed from the needs of reproduction' (Giddens, 1993: 2).

2.   These theorists include de Beauvoir, Kristeva, Irigaray, Wittig, Freud, Lacan and Foucault.

3.   Judith Butler argues that the horizons on which we act are not an external theatre of operations, but 'a constitutive possibility of our very capacity to act' (Butler, 1992a: 10).

4.   See Segal, 1994; Weeks, 1985, 1989.

INVESTIGATING SEX – ESSENTIALISM AND CONSTRUCTIONISM

Sexuality is highly contested. Its contestability opens the way for numerous strategies aimed at defining, explaining, and hence regulating, what 'the sexual' comprises.

Researchers have adopted different ways of thinking about, investigating and explaining 'the sexual'. The distinction most commonly made is between 'essentialist' and 'constructionist' approaches. Put another way, a distinction can be made between the perception that sexuality is a 'biological' phenomenon and the perception that it is a 'social' phenomenon.

Lynne Segal (1994) identifies three dominant paradigms in the history of Western approaches to sexual matters – the spiritual, the biological and the social.[1] According to Segal, in pre-industrial European societies, the regulation of sexual behaviour was primarily a spiritual and religious affair (Segal, 1994: 72). However, 'the sexual became synonymous with the biological' with the birth of the scientific study of sex and the usurpation of authority by doctors and scientists to speak of sexual normality and deviance. Scientific explanations of sex and sexuality have proved especially powerful and enduring. However, scientific paradigms have been seriously challenged, though not dismissed, in recent decades by the perception that nature and biology are social constructions and the notion that 'our experiences of the body and its desires are produced externally through the range of social discourses and institutions which describe and manipulate them' (Segal, 1994: 73).

A new way of thinking about sex does not completely replace a previous one, and different paradigms may coexist. Indeed, biological discourse – deploying scientific method and essentialist premises – has dominated perceptions of the body and sex/uality throughout the twentieth century. The uptake of a constructionist perspective in the social sciences has not meant the abandonment of the scientific study of sex in disciplines like psychology.

'Essentialism' entails the belief that sexuality is purely a natural phenomenon, outside of culture and society, made up of fixed and inherent drives, and that nature and these drives dictate our sexual identities

(Weeks, 1995). Sexuality is thus viewed as an instinctual, driving and potentially overwhelming force, which exerts an influence both on the individual and on culture. Essentialists tend to subscribe to the belief that sexual instinct, rightly or wrongly, is held in check by social, moral, medical mechanisms (Weeks, 1985). The individual is the subject of investigation and of necessary (for society to be possible) repressions. An essentialist model of sexuality unites different shades of political opinion, including that aimed at controlling (on the moral right) and liberating (on the left) sexuality (Weeks, 1989).

'Constructionism' entails the belief that sexuality has no inherent essence but must be understood as a configuration of cultural meanings which are themselves generated within matrices of social (power) relations (Gagnon and Parker, 1995; Segal, 1994; Weeks, 1995). Cultural institutions (like marriage and patriarchy), norms, practices and relations are the objects of study. Constructionist approaches have been explicitly concerned with power and politics – that is, the ways in which the construction of the sexual has the effect of privileging some sexual forms and denigrating others. However, ideas about the ways in which power 'works' through sexuality and constructs sexual identities and practices vary a great deal.

Essentialism and constructionism are not single political/theoretical positionings. Each is an 'umbrella' term which spans many differences in research agendas, perspectives and methodologies. The terms are themselves historically specific products of particular cultural, political and historical contexts. However, they can be contrasted in terms of a few broad assumptions about what the sexual comprises and how it is constituted.

Sexology and essentialism

'Sexology' is a term used to describe a range of historically specific endeavours directed at the 'scientific' study of sex. Gagnon and Parker (1995) describe what they call a 'sexological period', dating from 1890 to 1980, in which sex researchers and activists attempted to bring sexuality under the control of 'science'.

Sexologists in the late nineteenth century and early twentieth century were eager to reform sexuality, to oppose what were seen as repressive and restrictive doctrines and practices of the Victorian era (Gagnon and Parker, 1995: 5).[2] Sexological views were seen by the radicals and reformers of the time as liberating.

'Sexology' does not refer to a unified discipline or theoretical perspective. The generic term *science* tends to imply a closed and monolithic domain of knowledge, but this obscures the diversity of methods, problems and complexities addressed by different inquiries (Harding, S., 1986). Sexologists have used a variety of methods in the study of sexuality – from the clinical interview and life history up to the 1930s, to survey questionnaires and field studies of the 1940s to 1960s, laboratory observation and experimentation, in the 1960s and 1970s and ethnographic approaches in the 1970s (Gagnon and Parker, 1995: 6).

One approach is aimed at *describing* the diversity of existing sexual practices and preferences and concentrates on the collection of empirical data. Weeks describes this approach as 'naturalist', since it aims to describe, classify and categorise 'sexual forms that exist "in nature"' (Weeks, 1989: 2). A naturalist approach is typified in the late nineteenth-century sexological work of Havelock Ellis and has been evident in many large surveys of sexual attitudes and behaviours conducted since then.

For example, the scientific study of sex has been extended by the statistical analyses of the sexual behaviour of 12,000 white Americans based on detailed interviews produced by Albert Kinsey (Segal, 1994: 88); by surveys of 15,000 men's and women's experiences of sex conducted by Shere Hite between 1972 and 1986 (Hite, 1994); and, in 1994, by the publication of a report of a national survey of sexual attitudes and lifestyles of the British population based on statistical analysis of the interview responses of almost 20,000 randomly selected (to represent the views of the whole population) Britons (Wellings et al., 1994). Other descriptive work includes the ethnographic field work of social anthropologists. Many of these researchers (in particular Ellis and Kinsey) presented their data on the existence of diverse sexual forms and practices as evidence that they existed 'in nature' and were, therefore, not to be considered abnormal. Lynne Segal claims that Kinsey considered that which is natural to be healthy (learning from other mammals) (Segal, 1994: 88) and that 'his dogged determinism to disclose the variability and fluidity of sexual behaviour provided an important weapon for sexual minorities who, like Kinsey himself, wanted to abolish the distinction between "normal" and "abnormal" sexuality and insist that sexual conventions should encompass sexual realities' (Segal, 1994: 89).[3] Masters and Johnson studied what they called the human sexual response, defined as a distinctively physiological response, in an experimental study. They recorded 'the bodily contractions, secretions, pulse rates and tissue colour changes occurring during more than 10,000 male and female orgasms, produced in the laboratory by 694 white, middle-class heterosexual men and women' and defined women's sexual capacity as greater and more varied than men's (Segal, 1994: 93). These studies have produced a great deal of information but little explanation of the variations reported in sexual forms and how attitudes change. Other sexological studies of sexuality (usually derived from psychodynamic or neo-Freudian theory) have produced theories to explain the development of specific sexual forms, but have prioritised theoretical constructs over the collection of 'empirical evidence' (Weeks, 1989: 2).

Sexologists, despite considerable differences, have in common a commitment to producing a 'science of sex', and share several concerns and beliefs about sex. In particular, they subscribe to the idea that sex has an ultimately discoverable *essence*, insisting on the privileged role of sex in expressing 'the natural' and constituting 'sexuality as an "eternal duel" of the "unruly energy" and the constraints of "society"' (Weeks, 1985: 11). Sexologists agreed that 'sex was a natural force that existed in opposition to civilisation, culture or society' (Gagnon and Parker, 1995: 7). Cultures and societies were seen as responding to, rather than shaping, the sexual impulse. Thus, 'the individual and the drive were prior to the social or cultural order' (ibid.), and sexuality was a powerful and profound force. However, they were divided on whether the sex drive was 'a virtuous force warped by a negative civilisation (see Masters and Johnson, Kinsey, Mead, Ellis) or a negative force that required social control (see Freud and most of his followers)' (ibid.).

Even though sexologists were adamant in their attempts to 'explain the biological imperative of sex', they did acknowledge that social control and regulation varied within and across different cultures. They recognised 'different rules of marriage, monogamy, taboos against incest and responses to non-procreative sex even as they sought to naturalise them' (Weeks, 1985: 97). Sexologists held differing views with regard to how, and the degree to which, the expression of sexual instinct should be patrolled by social and cultural mechanisms and the possible consequences of particular social interventions (Wood, 1985: 157). The conduct of individuals was the focus of research because the drive was embedded in the individual.

Importantly, science, because of its claims to objectivity and impartiality, was seen to make the study of sex 'respectable' (whereas otherwise it had seemed distasteful). The scientific study of sex was justified by the belief that science was capable of producing 'an unbiased version of sexuality' which if understood and applied would reduce ignorance about sex and lead to 'human betterment' (Gagnon and Parker, 1995: 7). Sexologists shared a belief in 'the privileged character of positive scientific knowledge', which was seen as trans-cultural and trans-historical. Admittedly, there might be 'variations in cultural practices', but 'the underlying nature of sexuality remains the same in all times and places' (Gagnon and Parker, 1995: 7–8).

Nearly all theorists of 'the sexological period' believed that there were fundamental differences between the sexuality of men and of women – 'differences that followed upon the natural differences between the feminine and the masculine':

> As a corollary of these beliefs . . . theories of sexuality were normatively dominated by notions of men's sexuality and by heterosexual images and practices. (Gagnon and Parker, 1995: 7)

Sexual instinct was invested with a biologically ordained *aim* (intercourse) and *object* (usually a person of the opposite sex) (Wood, 1985). According to Segal, early sexologists 'saw male and female sexuality as fundamentally opposed: the one aggressive and forceful, the other responsive and maternal' (Segal, 1994: 76). Early sex researchers helped to affirm 'male domination as biological necessity, portraying "the sex act", understood as heterosexual genital engagement, as its exemplary moment' (Segal, 1994: 79).

These ideas were not uncontested. Whilst nineteenth-century feminists had been primarily concerned with 'protecting women from the dangers of male sexuality – disgrace, forced sex and unwanted pregnancy', many resisted the repressive culture of the time (Segal, 1994: 83). In the early part of the twentieth century, feminists like Stella Browne and Olive Schreiner argued for women's rights to the fulfilment of their sexuality on its own terms, which was seen as different from men's, and in this way helped to articulate new positions of desiring subjectivity for women (Browne, 1915; Rowbotham, 1977a: 87–90; Weeks, 1989: 167).

There has been a gradual shift in emphasis in twentieth-century sexo-logical discourse away from sexual difference and towards sameness. There has been increasing recognition of women's, as well as men's, capac-ity for sexual pleasure and a commitment to the idea that women could and should experience such pleasure. However, this is not to say that women's and men's sexual pleasures were seen as equivalent or that imbalances in the power relations of heterosexuality were being addressed:

> whether feminists demanded or decried the expression of women's desire for sex with men, metaphors of male conquest and female submission have remained, to this day, tied in with conceptions of heterosexuality. (Segal, 1994: 85)

Sexological discourse has been extremely influential in defining and explaining 'the sexual'. Sexology has achieved a privileged status, based on its claims to scientific and political rationality, and, consequently, has influ-enced many other social activities and institutions, including the law, medicine and social welfare agencies. The definitions produced within sexological discourse have had 'major effects in shaping our concepts of male and female sexuality, in demarcating the boundaries of the normal and abnormal, in defining the homosexual and other sexual "deviants"' (Weeks, 1985: 91).

However, the objectivity and impartiality claimed by sexologists have been challenged by the assertions that these definitions are themselves highly political and that sexological discourse has always been deeply entangled with other contemporary discourses: in particular, discourses on gender, race, class and nationality.

Challenges to essentialism

Essentialist accounts of sexuality, in which sexuality is seen as biologically given and socially repressed, have been challenged from several different theoretical perspectives within the last few decades.

Jeffrey Weeks (1989) suggests that the main theoretical challenges have been: 'the interactionist', 'the psychoanalytical' and 'the discursive' (Weeks, 1989: 3).[4] According to Weeks, despite their use of very different theoretical approaches, these challenges converge on several important themes. In particular, all of these approaches reject the idea that the sexual is an autonomous and rebellious realm which the social controls. From an inter-actionist perspective, it is suggested that 'nothing is intrinsically sexual' and 'anything can be sexualised' (Weeks, 1989: 3). In Lacan's reinterpreta-tion of Freud, sexuality is constituted in language. In Foucault's writing, sexuality is 'the name that can be given to a historical construct' (ibid.: 4). Anti-essentialist critiques are also linked by 'a recognition of the social and historical sources of sexual definitions' (ibid.).[5]

'Interests' have been crucial in the evolution of anti-essentialist approaches. Gagnon and Parker argue that by the 1960s

> it was clear that the sexological paradigm was in serious trouble, particularly at the level of explanation. . . . The important criticisms came from social scientists within sex research and from activist groups who were attempting to recon-struct central features of the paradigm that were prejudicial to their interests. (1995: 8)

Critics of sexology challenged 'both the universalist conception of the sexual as well as the privileged status of scientific inquiry' (ibid.). They argued that science was not unbiased.

Critical studies of science[6] and different feminist research programmes[7] have proliferated in recent decades to demonstrate the ways in which sci-ence can be considered 'biased'.

Sexologists' belief in the neutral, trans-cultural and trans-historical char-acter of scientific knowledge was countered with the claim that sexological knowledge was historically and culturally specific and also highly political in its generation and application. The concepts deployed in sexological discourse (for example, conceptions of the individual and the purpose of sexuality) reflected the uneven relations of gender, race and class. Further, it was argued that science did not reveal the truth about a naturally occur-ring sexuality 'out there'; instead it helped to construct it through the knowledge it produced, which legitimised some sexual practices and den-igrated others.[8] That is, cultural notions about the proper roles and functions of men and women have influenced scientific understandings of sex and sexuality (Jacobus et al., 1990; Martin, 1989, 1990; Poovey, 1990).

Many of the key categories used in sexology to describe and classify aspects of sexual life (like homosexuality, masculinity and femininity) have been shown not to be universal but highly localised (Gagnon and Parker, 1995: 11). Categories like 'sex', 'the body' and 'nature', the taken-for-granted trans-cultural and trans-historical bedrock of sexological research, have been deconstructed to show how they are the product, not the cause of contemporary cultural preoccupations. For example, it is widely believed in scientific and popular cultures that sex is a universal, ahistorical attribute of the body, and the basis of social and sexual behaviour. However, 'the sexed body' has been shown to be a changing idea in history, culture and discourse.[9] Historians have demonstrated that sex has been differently conceptualised by scientists at different historical moments and that their conceptualisations have reflected the contemporary social organisation of gender (Jacobus et al., 1990; Laqueur, 1990; Martin, 1989; Oudshoorn, 1994; Schiebinger, 1986). Scientists' conceptions of sex had the effect of 'naturalising' gender relations – that is, giving the impression that they were determined by an underlying 'nature' and so were inevitable. This was the result of scientists' claim that they could describe and explain 'nature' as it really was and represent nature as a force directing the world, to which the social responds. Scientists' descriptions of 'sex' were assumed to be an accurate record of that which existed in nature and dictated the social dimensions of gender. Not surprisingly, 'nature' has increasingly become the object of deconstruction.

The idea that sexuality is a 'natural' force, deriving from our biological being, has been extremely powerful in popular and scientific discourse and continues to be influential. Deployed as a key category in sexology, 'nature' has considerable rhetorical and persuasive power. It must then be asked: To what precisely do 'nature' and 'natural' refer?

'Nature' can be viewed as an idea in history whose meanings have changed over time. The idea that biological sex research is more basic than other approaches, because it examines something closer to nature and pre-social (and therefore more generalisable) can be traced to constructions of nature which served Enlightenment politics (Tiefer, 1995: 38).

Since the inception of what is often called 'The Enlightenment Project',[10] the natural world has been construed as the ideal object of intellectual endeavour and as the source of knowledge. The exercise of reason has been seen as the best way of producing an objective, reliable and universal foundation for knowledge (Flax, 1990: 41). It was thought that the knowledge produced through the correct use of reason would be 'true'. Science achieved a special significance and authority in modern societies because it was seen to exemplify the right use of reason, to enable a more rigorous and comprehensive commitment to the principles of objectivity, impartiality and independence, and to be impartial in method and content (Flax, 1990; Hall et al., 1992). Reason itself, considered to possess transcendental and universal qualities, was thought to exist 'independently of the self's contingent existence (e.g. bodily, historical, and social experiences do not affect reason's structure or its capacity to produce atemporal knowledge)' (Flax, 1990: 41). Thus, scientists claim to discover facts about 'nature' which are disinterested and true and, in doing so, to exert control over it (nature). The capacity of scientific discourse to effect such mastery relies upon and embodies a binary logic, comprising a series of conceptual dichotomies – culture vs. nature, mind vs. body, reason vs. emotion, objectivity vs. subjectivity – in which the former terms must dominate the latter

(Harding, S., 1986: 23). Some feminists have claimed that the former (dominating categories) are systematically associated with the masculine and the latter (subordinated categories) with the feminine.

Nature, according to Raymond Williams, is possibly the 'most complex word' in the English language (Williams, 1976: 184).[11] Williams traces the historical development of the word, discussing three uses of the word 'nature'. The first meaning, from the thirteenth century, is 'the essential quality and character *of* something'; the second, from the fourteenth century, is 'the inherent force which directs either the world or human beings or both'; the third, from the seventeenth century, is 'the material world itself, taken as including or not including human beings'. The latter use has retained currency and nature is used to mean the countryside ('the "unspoiled" places, plants and creatures other than man') in distinguishing between town and country (Williams, 1976: 186).

In *Sex Is Not a Natural Act*, Leonore Tiefer examines Williams's history of the meanings of nature in relation to sexological research. She argues that 'the term *nature* is often used in sexology for its rhetorical power'. By emphasizing that something is *in nature*, a sense of solidity and validity is conferred. This use calls on nature *in contrast with culture*, implying that anything human-made is 'false', whereas something outside of human culture is 'true'. 'Sexual nature', Tiefer writes, sounds 'like something solid and valid, not human-made' (Tiefer, 1995: 32, 33).

Deconstruction/ reconstruction

Constructionism meant, among other things, that it was theoretically possible to deconstruct and reconstruct popular and scientific conceptions of sexuality.

Within the framework of what Weeks calls the 'new social histories', sexuality was understood as a variable category of experience and was constituted in relation to, and in interaction with, other historically and culturally variable social practices (legal, biomedical, religious, economic) and relations (class, race and gender). These practices and relations also helped to generate categories and concepts which organise sexuality and define grids of tolerance and intolerance towards, for example, teenage pregnancy and sex outside of marriage, openly declared homosexuality, prostitution and children's sexual knowledge. (In)tolerance is based on definitions of what is considered healthy and unhealthy, normal and abnormal, appropriate and inappropriate in sexual life formulated within the same practices and relations (Weeks, 1985: 7).

The 'naturalness' of contemporary sexuality, gender roles and sexual attitudes was also undermined by the radical movements of the 1970s (in particular the women's movement and the lesbian and gay movement) (Segal, 1994; Weeks, 1985). If sex felt individual and private, individuality and privacy were *ideas* which also incorporated the roles, definitions, symbols and meanings of the worlds in which they were constructed: they were culturally and historically contingent.

'The personal is the political' was the feminist slogan which encapsulated this insight. Feminists argued that prevailing patterns of subordination and domination in society at large were reproduced in the most intimate sphere of private life, that of sexual relations. Moreover, these relations were sustained by *social* definitions of female sexuality disguised as descriptions of 'essential' female sexuality. Most importantly, feminists have revealed the interconnections of power and sexuality and therefore made sexual politics a central aspect of everyday life and the social and political relations which organise it (Weeks, 1985; Wood, 1985).

The critical contribution of feminist studies to sex research was, according to Gagnon and Parker, 'the recognition that gender was a larger frame through which sexuality in Western societies should be interpreted' (1995: 8). Feminist studies drew attention to the 'facts' that men did most of the research on sex, that the sexuality of men was taken to be the norm (against which all else was compared), that sexual practices of women and men were determined by inequalities in power, and that the relation of gender to sexuality was not fixed (1995: 8–9).

Lesbian and gay studies drew attention to variable and complex relations between identity and behaviour and showed that categories like '"homosexual", "bisexual", and "heterosexual", "gay", "queer", and "clone" are all social constructs which are ambiguously tied to behaviour' (Gagnon and Parker, 1995a). These insights also have implications for race, gender and class issues 'in which public performances are often tied to private identities' (Gagnon and Parker, 1995a). Identity categories are explored further in relation to cultural politics, constructionism and essentialism in Chapter 4.

Lesbian and gay critiques of sexology have shown 'the increased importance of self-identified lesbian and gay researchers in doing research on lesbian and gay issues' (Gagnon and Parker, 1995: 9). Gays had previously been excluded from studying gays on the grounds of likely bias, whilst it was not recognised that heterosexuals would be biased (more so perhaps because of homophobia). The emergence of gay researchers implied a significant critique 'both of the positivist ideal of unbiased research and of the idea that same-gender sexual practices are abnormal' (Gagnon and Parker, 1995: 10). Ironically, the consequences of these developments may be more conservative than radical.

Women's studies and lesbian and gay studies have carved out new fields of study and have been successful because men and heterosexuals have given over this territory. In doing so, these dominant groups have been able to avoid in part 'an analysis of men as gendered creatures as well as an analysis of the socially constructed nature of contemporary heterosexuality' (Gagnon and Parker, 1995: 10). A continued focus on the gender/ sexualities of non-dominant groups (even though women and gays may be the researchers) makes these into problems and leaves the masculine and heterosexual undeconstructed as the norm.

Social constructionists held that sexuality was not 'based on internal drives, but was elicited in specific historical and social circumstances' (Gagnon and Parker, 1995: 8). The constructionist view was that we can only understand sexuality through the cultural meanings which construct it (Weeks, 1995). This approach does not assume that biology is unimportant, nor that individuals are simply blank sheets on which society writes its cultural messages. According to Weeks, it is not a question of whether, for example, homosexuality is inborn or learned, but of the meanings that a particular culture 'gives to homosexual behaviour, however it may be caused, and what are the effects of those particular meanings on the ways in which individuals organise their lives' (Weeks, 1995: 34). Weeks suggests that this is a historical and a highly political question – one, which concerns *not* the true nature of identities but identities' political relevance. Thus, Weeks argues that where it is commonly believed that sexuality is the least changeable amongst social phenomena, this is an effect of ideology which makes 'us believe that what is socially created, and therefore subject to change, is really natural, and therefore immutable' (ibid.).

Setting the scene for *Sex Acts*

Deconstruction is never complete. The logic of constructionism is that all knowledge production is political in the sense that it is intimately bound up with power relations. Constructionists' researchs and explanations are also constructed.

Feminist, lesbian and gay studies of sexuality have undoubtedly posed important and interesting challenges to the orthodoxies of sexological discourse. Because of the theoretical/political underpinnings of this work, Gagnon and Parker argue, it has tended to be historical, since 'it is difficult to be constructionist when engaged in social resistance since constructionism emphasises the temporary character of both oppressors and revolutionaries' (Gagnon and Parker, 1995: 10). One effect of this has been to formulate identities and sexualities as self-evident categories to be liberated from previous constraints and oppressions and, simultaneously, to tend towards essentialising such sexual identities. As a way of 'getting at' the present and the contingencies of identity categories, I pitch my analysis of sexuality at the level of discourse.

In *Sex Acts* I view sexuality *as* discourse. Several points motivate this approach. Firstly, the 'hold' that science appears to have on 'truth', and the widespread popular appeal of this and the security it provides, is deeply entrenched in modern Western cultures. By viewing science as one of a number of plausible discourses, which are culturally and historically located, it is possible to thoroughly question (rather than simply reproduce and reinforce) its terms of reference. It is possible to reveal some of the cultural meanings underpinning scientific statements and open the way for producing alternative (possibly less constraining) meanings.

Secondly, whilst some anti-essentialist approaches developed by theorists/activists in response to aspects of the sexological paradigm prejudicial to their 'interests' have given rise to the description and celebration (rather than denigration) of sexualities these have not been subjected to the same level of critique. That is, these (newly 'liberated') sexualities have not always been viewed as also historically contingent. My point here is that sexuality can never be separated from power, so there can be no truly free or liberated sexuality – just new configurations of 'the sexual' within power relations which also cannot help but regulate subjects (albeit in different ways). This is not to say that some forms of regulation might not be preferable to others and less constraining for some. A focus on sexuality as discourse requires that the political discourses of particular self-identified collectivities (feminist, lesbian, gay) also be scrutinised to reveal the ways in which they construct sexual identities in specific historical and cultural circumstances.

Thirdly, ideas about sexuality are complex and hybrid: they do not necessarily belong to one paradigm or another but circulate and are borrowed and modified, whether consciously or unconsciously, by different researchers/activists. Analysis of discourse – involving a detailed examination of what gets said, by whom and from where – is one way of working beyond the limits of specific disciplines to discover how specific ideas come about and their effects (deconstruction) and to think about other ways in which sex might be put into words, and for which purposes (reconstruction).

Working at the level of discourse, as Foucault (1986) conceptualises it, will facilitate my looking at the ways in which sexualities are shaped and organised in the 1990s. This approach provides an effective means of deconstructing powerful ideas and theories – those of science and those of political 'identity politics'.

Foucault, sex and discourse

In *The History of Sexuality* (1981), Foucault discusses the relations between sex, power and discourse. Sexuality, for Foucault, is historically and discursively constructed within relations of power. There is no essential human quality (sexuality) to be repressed or liberated. Rather, there are ideas about sexuality which are put into words – discourses.[12] Weeks reads this as meaning that 'the sexual only exists in and through the modes of its organisation and representation' (1985: 10) – that is, through aesthetic, scientific, historical and political discourses. Sexuality has no reality outside of these discourses, which claimed merely to describe it but actually construct it. The history of sexuality in the West is actually the history of discourses on sexuality. Sexuality is then the endpoint of discourses which attempt to define it, analyse it, control it, emancipate it (Weeks, 1989).

Foucault argues that sex has been volubly and excessively spoken about in modern societies since the seventeenth century, as part of the processes of modern power (Foucault, 1981). Contrary to popular belief, the Victorian era was not a time of repression of sexuality in the West, which could then be liberated in the twentieth century. Instead, Foucault argues, far from being repressed or restricted, discourse on sex has been 'subjected to a mechanism of increasing excitement' (1981: 12). The explosion of discourses on sex can be seen as part of a complex extension of social control over the individual through the apparatus of sexuality (Weeks, 1989). Discourses have issued from a variety of institutions (medical, religious, legal, psychiatric, educational) and these discourses have *constructed* sexuality (as residing in organs, endowed with instincts, leading a separate life in the inner recesses of the individual).

Modern societies have been inclined to define the relation between sex and power as one of repression, whereby sex is considered in need of liberation. This definition may be particularly gratifying because if sex is repressed and condemned to silence, then the mere act of speaking about it has 'the appearance of a deliberate transgression' (Foucault, 1981: 7). Someone who talks about sex in this way appears to be 'outside the reach of power' and is conscious of defying power (ibid.). Contemporary representations of sexualities may be transgressive, because they dare to speak out about sex and name its unacceptable – adulterous, criminal, perverse – forms. In this sense, someone who, for example, 'comes out' or attempts to 'out' someone else is exercising a degree of power. They may also help to constitute and reinforce a boundary between public and private domains, even as they appear to erase it.

According to Weeks, what is ultimately significant in Foucault's work is his 'recognition of the constant struggles within the definition of sexuality'. Thus, he rejects the concept of 'liberation' and maintains that sexual radicalism should not try to free a repressed essence but to consciously intervene 'at the level of the definition of appropriate sexual behaviour' (Weeks, 1989: 10).

Analysis of discourse

'Discourse analysis' refers to a method of investigating the social construction of phenomena, including ideas, practices and domains of knowledge. According to Foucault, 'discourse' constitutes social phenomena (Foucault, 1979, 1981, 1986). Discourses are *practices*, rather than structures or superstructures, that are lived, acted out and spoken by individuals. Discourses operate as fields of fluid and mobile 'relations' and 'interrelations' which produce and transmit knowledge and power relations (Foucault, 1979, 1986).

In Foucault's texts, power and knowledge directly imply one another. Thus, 'there is no power relation without the correlative constitution of a field of knowledge, nor any knowledge, that does not presuppose and constitute at the same time power relations' (Foucault, 1979: 27). Knowledge does not derive from some subject of knowledge but from the power relations, the processes and struggles, that traverse and invest it. The important point about Foucault's concept of power is that it is not a property but a strategy that is exercised from 'innumerable points in the interplay of non egalitarian and mobile relations' (Foucault, 1981: 94) and is met with a 'multiplicity of points of resistance' (ibid.: 95). In this way, Foucault conceptualises power as positive (meaning that it is creative), rather than negative (meaning that it is constraining).

Discourses, according to Foucault (1986) are comprised of statements which must be spoken from somewhere and by someone, and this speaking entails the *bringing into being* and positioning of a subject and assignment of a 'subject position'. The idea of 'subject positions' located within the historical contingencies of a specific discourse, spoken from a particular time and place, replaces the idea of a hegemonic knowing subject or coherent subjectivity which exists before and across discourses. Within this framework, emphasis is placed on examining particular statements to ascertain who is speaking from where, of what, and how it is possible to create new statements, subjects and speaking positions. For any individual, subjectivity is not coherent nor complete but must be repeatedly (re)signified in and through discourse, involving the assignment and adoption of different positions of subjectivity.

The objects of discourse and discourse itself emerge in the same process (Foucault, 1986: 45). Discourses systematically form and order, within relations of power, the objects of which they speak. This conceptualisation does not involve denying a prediscursive existence for the subject nor for the objects of discourse. Rather, whether or not object and subjects exist outside of discourse, they are constituted as such within discourse (Laclau and Mouffe, 1985: 108). Within this framework, even their prediscursive existence is produced in discourse.[13]

In the following chapters, I emphasise the productive and organising functions of discourse in order to show how sex/ualities are made and might be remade, and how specific discursive constructions of 'the sexual' create some sexual subject positions and foreclose others. I look at how different (sometimes conflicting) discourses intersect to address and 'position' sexual subjects and the ways in which these 'positionings' may be resisted. This approach opens up more room for manoeuvre (theoretically/politically speaking) than one which is based on the idea of a repressed/liberated sexuality.

Notes

1. 'A paradigm is composed of an interrelated set of accepted explanations, methods and observations' (Gagnon and Parker, 1995: 8).

2. According to Gagnon and Parker, the following were key names in sexology:

Freud and his followers, Ellis, Hirshfield, Malinowski, Stopes, Sanger, Guyon, Reich, Mead, Kinsey and his associates, and Masters and Johnson (Gagnon and Parker, 1995: 5).

3. 'For example, he reported that at least 37% of the thousands of American males he interviewed had some homosexual experience' (Segal, 1994: 89).

4. According to Weeks (1989) 'the interactionist' is associated with the work of Gagnon and Simon and Plummer. See Gagnon and Simon, 1973. 'The psychoana-lytical' is associated with Jacques Lacan's reinterpretation of Freud and has subsequently been taken up by feminists like Juliet Mitchell. See Mitchell, 1975 and also Mitchell and Rose, 1982. 'The discursive' is primarily associated with the work of Michel Foucault and especially *The History of Sexuality. Volume One* (Foucault, 1981).

5. See Weeks (1989: 4–6) for a fuller discussion of the key differences between these challenges to essentialist views.

6. These include studies of/in science, the history of science, the philosophy of science and feminist critiques of science. Critiques are extremely diverse, employ-ing different methods, conceptualising different problems and coming up with different conclusions. See the collected essays on: 'science' by Latour (1983), Latour and Woolgar (1979), Rose and Rose (1976), Knorr-Cetina and Mulkay (1983); and 'gender and science' by Haraway (1990, 1991), Rose (1983, 1994), Kirkup and Smith Keller (1992), Harding and O'Barr (1987), Keller (1983, 1985, 1987), Keller and Grontkowski (1983), Tuana (1989), Dugdale (1988), Hubbard (1988), Imber and Tuana (1988), Blier (1984), Harding and Hintikka (1983), Harding, J. (1986), Hubbard et al. (1982), Harding, S. (1986, 1990), Harvey (1989), Schiebinger (1987). See also specialist journals, for example *Philosophy of Social Science, Studies in the History of Biology, Social Studies of Science, The Philosophical Forum, Bulletin of the History of Medicine, Journal of Medicine and Philosophy, Journal of the History of Biology, Signs: Journal of Women in Culture and Society 6 (no.3)*.

7. Sandra Harding (1986) distinguishes five research programmes aimed at challenging 'gender bias' in science: (1) 'equity studies' examining the barriers to women's participation in science; (2) 'studies of the uses and abuses of biology, the social sciences and their technologies' which have revealed 'the ways in which science is used in the services of sexist, racist, homophobic and classist social pro-jects' (e.g. reproductive policies, medical cures for homosexuals) (Harding, S., 1986: 21) (the assumption here is that there can be a value-free science, pure scientific research that can be distinguished from the social uses of science); (3) usual science as 'bad science', based on the idea that the selection and definition of problematics have been skewed towards men's problems (not women's) and explanations of men's gender desires and needs, i.e. the design and interpretation of research is masculine biased (as if it could be other than value laden) (Harding, S., 1986: 22); (4) 'reading science as text' (using techniques of literary criticism, historical interpre-tation and psychoanalysis) – this is directed at revealing 'the social meanings – the hidden semiotic and structural agendas – of purportedly value-neutral claims and practices' (ibid.: 23). This includes drawing out 'metaphors of gender politics' and viewing the 'rigid series of dichotomies in science and epistemology' ('objectivity vs. subjectivity, the scientist as the knowing subject vs. the object of his inquiry, reason vs. the emotions, mind vs. body', in which 'the former has been associated with masculinity and the latter with femininity' and it has been claimed that 'human progress requires the former to achieve domination of the latter': ibid.) *not* as 'a reflection of the progressive character of scientific inquiry', rather, as

'inextricably connected with specifically masculine – perhaps uniquely Western and bourgeois – needs and desires' (ibid.); (5) 'feminist epistemological inquiries' which form a basis for understanding how 'beliefs are grounded in social experiences, and of what kind of experience ground the beliefs we honor as knowledge' (ibid.: 24).

8. Nelly Oudshoorn (among others) states very clearly the view that, rather than discovering facts about reality 'out there', scientists are engaged in the collective creation of statements constituting reality (Oudshoorn, 1994).

9. See Chapter 3 for a fuller discusion of this.

10. 'The Enlightenment Project' refers to an intellectual and philosophical movement originating in the eighteenth century and comprising clusters of assumptions and expectations, sets of ideas and themes, that occurred 'at the threshold of typically modern Western society' (McLennan, G., 1992).

11. 'Any full history of the uses of *nature* would be a history of a large part of human thought' (Williams, 1976: 186). 'Nature' conveys many of the variations in human thought over time and all its meanings are in use, often together (ibid.: 189).

12. Foucault is interested in the way in which 'sex is put into discourse' and 'the discourses it permeates in order to reach the most tenuous and individual modes of behaviour' and how it 'penetrates and controls everyday pleasure', all of which constitute 'polymorphous techniques of power' (Foucault, 1981: 11).

13. This does not necessarily involve a rejection of those critiques which address 'the subject' as a prediscursive entity, but may in some ways complement this significant field of inquiry. I am thinking particularly of feminist psychoanalytic critiques of, and attempts to destabilise, the (masculine) subject: including those based in object relations (Chodorow, 1978; Dinnerstein, 1978); and those which, in very different ways, take Lacanian psychoanalytic theory as a point of departure (Mitchell, 1975; Rose, 1986; Kristeva, 1982, 1986; Irigaray, 1985, 1988); and also French feminists' *écriture feminine* (Marks and de Courtivron, 1981). See also Judith Butler (1990b) for a discussion of how many feminist attempts at destabilising the (masculine) subject tend, nevertheless, to effect 'a false stabilisation of the category of women' (Butler, 1990b: 329).

3

PRIVATE SEX, PUBLIC DANGER

Crossing over

Sexuality is constantly spotlighted for a public gaze, yet it is considered to be the most personal and intimate of experiences. Even where the act of 'having sex' appears to be part of the public domain – in pornographic films and magazines, live sex shows, cottaging – a sense of the private persists, either in viewing these acts as exceptional or in the idea that irreducibly personal and undisclosed elements are present, like individual responses and fantasies.

The very idea of 'private' and 'public' as separate spheres appears to be central to understandings of what sexuality is. Sexuality in turn helps to demarcate the private and the public as discrete and separate domains, through various instances in which it 'crosses over', ceasing to be merely a private act and becoming a matter of public concern. This is most apparent when specific sexual outcomes (like pregnancy and HIV/AIDS) are construed as socially undesirable and specific groups are positioned as (potential) sexual transgressives (single women, teenagers, gays) through a variety of discourses (medical, public health, moral, right-wing political). These positionings may then occasion interventions like sex education and public health promotion activities directed at modifying individual sexual behaviour. Moving from the private into the public domain has historically had a political endpoint in emancipatory discourses – coming out as lesbian or gay, participating in 1970s-style feminist consciousness raising groups. The popularly held view that sex today is talked about more openly than in the past exerts some pressure on the private/public divide. The meanings of the private and public may alter, and the border constituting them as such may shift, but they remain significant. There is always a sense that one might intrude on the other.

Breastfeeding in public is surprisingly transgressive. Breastfeeding may represent a moment of shared pleasure and intimacy enjoyed by babies and mothers. Doing it in public for the first time, a woman may sense the discomfort of others and feel uncomfortable herself. In many situations, this practice is only barely tolerated (breastfeeding women may be asked to leave cinema foyers, and restaurants and large department stores provide secluded areas for women to feed their babies).

New mothers are addressed by competing discourses. They are encouraged to breastfeed on the grounds that breastfeeding gives infants the best possible nutrition, protects them against infections like gastroenteritis, and strengthens bonding between mother and baby. At the same time, they are deterred from doing it in public and impelled to think of it as a private (sex) act. Through these discourses, breastfeeding is inscribed as a 'natural' and 'domestic' (sex) act. Breastfeeding in public occasions the configuration of a maternal body through a heterosexualising gaze which also assigns sexuality to the home.

These ideas had a public airing during a 'world breastfeeding week' in 1996, when breastfeeding was also shown to be an historically and culturally contingent sex act. A journalist writing in the *Independent on Sunday* (Hunt, 1996) drew attention to a British Tourist Authority leaflet advising tourists that breastfeeding in public is not acceptable in Britain. Whilst health visitors, midwives and support groups responded angrily that this undermined breastfeeding initiatives and contravened government policy,[1] the Tourist Authority spokesman said that the leaflet was produced in response to complaints it had received from tourists saying that they felt embarrassed when breastfeeding in public in Britain (Hunt, 1996). *Who* is so intolerant?

Men, it is claimed, object most to women breastfeeding in front of them.[2] Hunt suggests that 'while British men abroad will reveal all at the first ray of sunshine, and spend hours ogling bare-breasted women on the beach, they draw the line when it comes to one of the most natural acts in the world'. Husbands and fathers feel most strongly, perhaps because they do not like their partners revealing parts of their bodies in public and do not see why other women should. How do mothers with new babies become so sexualised in public, when motherhood is not often regarded as sexy?

It appears that the slightest glimpse of mammary flesh provokes a reference to women's bodies which configures them as saturated with sexuality. Breasts, in particular, have been eroticised and fetishised in Western cultures. Breasts are constituted as sexual organs which, since sex is supposed to be private, are meant to be hidden – except in designated places of public display like some newspapers, magazines or sex shows. By breastfeeding in public women reveal (small parts of) their breasts to a public gaze and eroticisation, and render them (temporarily) public property. Some partners may feel that their sense of 'ownership' is overtly challenged. An apparent discomforting display of sexuality which causes dis-ease readily gets seen as unnatural.

If women are addressed and positioned by conflicting constructions of breastfeeding in public as natural yet pathological, do they recognise themselves in these 'interpellations'? How do they respond?

They may be oblivious to hostile looks, or they may decide to 'brazen it out' or to retreat into less public spaces like cars or the Ladies. Some public places may seem more hostile than others, like trains bursting with commuters. Women themselves may experience breastfeeding as erotic and sense that they are doing something intimate, personal and pleasurable in public. This is not to say that all men and women respond in a similar or negative way to breastfeeding women.

What are the effects of discourse which vigorously asserts breastfeeding as a natural bodily function ('one of the most natural acts in the world' (Hunt, 1996)), necessary to the healthy growth of babies? How does the naturalisation of breastfeeding as a direct, healthy and celebrated expression of the (already naturalised) maternal body position women who (for whatever reason) do not breastfeed? Are they unnatural or do they simply evade this particular example of naturalisation?

Discourses on breastfeeding constitute differently positioned feminine subjects within the narrow constraints of the natural/pathological and reinscribe the biological body as the basis of female sexuality. However, the category 'natural' is problematic and needs to be challenged.

Female sexuality is naturalised and domesticated through the spectacle of breastfeeding. Women breastfeeding in public are mostly obliged to 'resignify' themselves as acquiescent (to public pressure) or as transgressive.[3] An 'in yer face' approach to breastfeeding may produce new political subjects, who seek to create a space in which it is possible to do what is asserted as 'natural' and, possibly, provoke an idealised series of events in which visibility leads to familiarity which leads to increased public tolerance.

'Visibility' is a political issue. Visibility connotes being in the public eye and, as a result, open to scrutiny and judgement, leading to positive and negative evaluations. It also connotes power and ownership. Visibility, it is argued, has been a factor in arguments about both the oppression and the liberation of some cultural groups. Visibility has helped to extend social control over some subjects – for example women, some racial groups, the criminal and the sick – with the use of photography (discussed later in this chapter). Others have argued that cultural groups whose experiences have been left out of official histories have been rendered invisible and that this is a result of, and contributes to, their continuing oppression. The antidote, it is claimed, is to tell their stories and to make them visible (to give them a sense of their identities rooted in the past) as part of a process of empowerment and developing a stake in the future. That is, 'people(s) in the present need antecedents to locate themselves now and legitimate their ongoing and future ways of living' (Jenkins, 1991: 18).

In the rest of this chapter I examine the historical emergence of a private/public distinction as an idea in relation to the sexual and visual culture.

The historical emergence of the private and the public

What are the investments (historical and cultural) in the idea of the private as distinct from the public?

To begin with, a private/public distinction appears to be coextensive with other 'modern' distinctions – in particular, distinctions between mind and body, reason and passion, masculine and feminine. Social historians have identified a sharp separation of the world of work from that of family life; of the public sphere outside the home from the private sphere within the home, which has become particularly intense and *highly gendered* in the development of capitalist societies.

> Our lives have come to be organized around two realms: a private realm where women are most in evidence, where 'natural' functions like sex and the bodily functions related to procreation take place, where the affective content of relationships is primary, and a public realm where men are most in evidence, where 'culture' (books, schools, art, music, science) is produced, where money is made, work is done, and where one's efficiency at producing goods or services takes precedence over one's feelings about fellow workers. (Martin, 1989: 16)

The evolution of these two spheres in the nineteenth century has been the object of much detailed research (Alexander, 1976; Davidoff and Westover, 1986; Martin, 1989; Poovey, 1989; Rowbotham, 1977b; Walkowitz, 1982; Weeks, 1989) and some researchers argue that they persist today (Martin, 1989). Broadly speaking, it is argued that a distinctive private/public division emerged during industrialisation, when 'productive activity moved from the household to factories' and, increasingly, people worked for wages (Martin, 1989: 16).

Women's experience was differentiated by class: working-class women went into the labour market to earn wages, whereas middle-class women 'retreated into the home', where they were to cultivate 'the art of femininity'. Nineteenth-century bourgeois femininity consisted of 'abstinence' – from labour and sexuality – and reproduction (Martin, 1989: 16). That is, the function of the wife (in all except the poorest class) was to bear children, look after the house and keep her husband company. The social importance of the wife lay in her idleness, and non-productivity was an indicator of social standing. These supposedly distinctive and discrete spheres were not regarded equally – being productive in the world of paid work counted for more than being dependent in the domestic sphere (Martin, 1989: 16).

Sexual discourses in the late nineteenth century made a clear link between the private and the public via notions of 'health' – physical and moral. Public health depended on the regulation of individual conduct and moral reformation.

> Victorian morality was premised on a series of ideological separations: between family and society, between the restraint of the domestic circle and the temptations of promiscuity; between the privacy, leisure and comforts of the home and the tensions and competitiveness of work. And these divisions in social organisation and ideology were reflected in sexual attitudes. The decency and morality of the home confronted the danger and pollution of the public sphere; the joys and the 'naturalness' of the home countered the 'corruption', the artificiality of

the streets, badly lit, unhygenic, dangerous and immoral. This was the basis of the dichotomy of the 'private' and 'the public' upon which much sexual regulation rested. . . . The private was the nest of domestic virtues: the public was the arena of prostitution, of vice on the streets. (Weeks, 1989: 81)

Prostitution was, according to Weeks, of immense 'symbolic importance' to the Victorians and 'the main focus of the debate and moral reforming efforts from the 1850s onwards'. 'A widespread fear of the social implications of prostitution' is suggested by the frequent use at the time of terms such as 'social evil' and the 'social diseases' (Weeks, 1989: 84, 85).

Prostitution represented 'the other' for 'respectable' (middle-class) married womanhood and had a direct effect on sexuality within marriage. One of the ways in which this was evident was in the stigma conferred on artificial contraception. It was widely believed that prostitutes had a special knowledge of contraception, which led to it being designated 'immoral' (Gordon, 1977: 110–17; Weeks, 1989). For some time, the rejection of contraception became part of the production and regulation of respectable married womanhood (Harding, J., 1993). Eventually, in the twentieth century, the social stigma attached to artificial contraception gave way to publicly expressed anxieties about the health, quality and quantity of the population in the face of high maternal mortality, poverty and disease and the possibility of an absolute decline in population following the First World War (Weeks, 1989: 189).

Sexuality, during the nineteenth century, had become *symbolic* of wider social features. According to Weeks, this was perhaps the major contribution of the nineteenth century to twentieth-century discourse on sexuality. Major social disruptions were deflected onto the sphere of sexuality (Weeks, 1989: 92–3). This process was deeply gendered.

Some feminists argue that women's bodies have been consistently constructed, in nineteenth- and twentieth-century discourses, in terms of impulsive and unruly internal bodily processes which represent a continual source of potential disruption to the social order (Shuttleworth, 1990; Smart, 1992; Zita, 1988). These writers argue that the various discourses which have brought into being a problematic and radically unstable feminine subject have also produced *simultaneously* a self-evident need for its surveillance and regulation (Smart, 1992: 8). Their analyses are founded on the premises that, firstly, the unsteady oscillations of women's bodies represent *metonymically* the uncertain flux of contemporary economic and social spheres (Shuttleworth, 1990: 54–5); secondly, that an impulsive feminine body is an element in, productive of and produced by, a disciplinary society deploying various regulatory practices to achieve a desired docility (Smart, 1992: 31); and, thirdly, that the construction of women in bodily terms, helplessly subject to the tyranny of their bodies and in need of medical supervision, has functioned as a necessary support for the idea of its opposite: *autonomous man*, transcending his body by his capacity for rational thought, his own master, his health dependent on self-control and self-help (Shuttleworth, 1990: 64). Thus, Shuttleworth argues that the perception that mid-Victorian British women were 'in possession of a disruptive sexuality that needed to be disciplined and controlled' (ibid.: 54), signified above all by the flow of menstruation, represented not a need to control women and feminine sexuality *per se*, but *men's* problems in adapting to new conditions of the labour market and maintaining their mastery of the circulation of money in the economic sphere.

Scientific discourses of the day, and the metaphors used to describe and explain men's and women's bodies, helped to ground the doctrine of two spheres and the imbalance in contemporary gender relations in biology and nature (Martin, 1989).

Researchers have demonstrated that the metaphors used in scientific writing reflect and reproduce the values and relations of the time – in particular, the social organisation of gender and economy (Laqueur, 1990; Martin, 1989; Schiebinger, 1986). The concept 'sex', far from being an ahistorical, incontrovertible, universal attribute of the body which medical science reveals and describes, has been shown to have a history (scientists have conceptualised sex in different ways in different historical times). Indeed, science has been shown to be a *sexualising* discourse, which 'produces' the ideas of sex it claims to describe and naturalises these (see also Chapter 2).

Several researchers agree with Thomas Laqueur that the notion of difference between male and female bodies and sexualities is a relatively recent idea and very much related to the differentiation of private and public spheres (Laqueur, 1990; Martin, 1989; Oudshourn, 1994; Segal, 1994).

Prior to the late eighteenth century, medical literature represented male and female bodies as structurally similar – women had the same genitals as men, except that theirs were on the inside and not the outside. Structural similarity did not connote equality because the female body was constituted as a variation on a singular masculine model, its characteristics a copy of the basic male pattern, reflecting a male-dominated public sphere in which 'man is the measure of all things, and woman does not exist as an ontologically distinct entity' (Laqueur, 1990: 62). By 1800, according to Laqueur (1987), this logic and model was coming under devastating attack. Writers of all sorts were determined to base what they insisted were fundamental differences between male and female sexuality, and therefore between man and woman, on 'discoverable biological differences' (Martin, 1989: 31). Anatomists, biologists and physiologists increasingly focused on bodily differences, gradually sexualising parts of the body – starting with the skeleton (Schiebinger, 1986), and encompassing cells, brains and almost every part of the body (Oudshoorn, 1994). Male and female bodies became conceptualised in terms of opposites possessing 'incommensurably different organs, functions and feelings' (Laqueur, 1990: viii). These explanations of sexual difference were thought to 'prove' that the pattern of male–female relations that characterised the English middle classes was natural and inevitable. Gendered explanations of sex and sexuality legitimised the doctrine of two spheres – men as workers in the public, wage-earning sphere and women (except in the lower classes) as wives and mothers in the private, domestic sphere of kinship and morality. Even in the lower classes, where women were often forced to labour outside the home, this gendered organisation of private/public space constituted an ideal to which many (men) would aspire as part of establishing their own respectability.

The radical departure of the nineteenth century was that these explanations of sex and sexuality were accompanied by the denigration of uniquely female bodily processes which were defined in a hierarchical and pathological relation to maleness. Whereas menstrual blood was previously seen as simply impure, nineteenth-century writers stress the debilitating nature of menstruation and its pathology (Martin, 1989). Menstruation was seen as the external barometer of women's internal physical and mental health and signified women's greater susceptibility to bodily processes, particularly their unstable reproductive functions, which were seen to influence their whole bodies and entire lives (Laqueur, 1990; Martin, 1989; Shuttleworth, 1990; Smart, 1992). Women were always at the mercy of their wombs and debilitating menstrual flow.

Thus, sexuality in men and women was considered to be different. Women were shackled to 'an essentially destructive and demanding reproductive biology', which disqualified them from higher education, most professions and all aspects of public life:

> Women were never free from the pressures of their sex, always in danger of provoking male sexual arousal, although essentially self-sacrificing and passive. They were *the* sex, and yet in most Victorian thinking, curiously, themselves asexual. (Segal, 1994: 75)

Since the nineteenth century women have been seen as incomplete adults and inferior to men, on the grounds that they lack control over their bodies and emotions, which at various historical junctures have been seen as being under the sway of their uteruses or ovaries (Laqueur, 1987), or hormones (Harding, J., 1993; Oudshoorn, 1994; Vines, 1993). In late twentieth-century western culture, the medically constructed hormonal body operates as a blueprint for the natural and female body. Premenstrual, menopausal and pregnant women are widely believed to be controlled by their hormones and therefore to lack self-control and rationality.

The modern subject and the embodiment of desire

Sexuality is deeply implicated in modern constructions of subjectivity. The creation of the modern self is intimately linked to the body and, consequently, to sexuality, as the most corporeal of processes.

The concept of the modern subject is derived from Enlightenment ideas in which mind and body are conceived as separate entities. Mind is held to dominate the body, which is represented as an unruly mass of impulses, desires and emotions. As many theorists readily point out, this distinction is linked to and replicated in a series of other differentiations: of reason from passion, public from private, reality from appearance, culture from nature, humanity from animality, male from female, self from other (Grosz, 1994; Lupton, 1995a; Turner, 1984). The body is seen as a possession of mind, subject to the control of external forces and in need of discipline and training. Thus, 'if the body appears uncontrolled then the self is revealed as undisciplined' (Lupton, 1995a: 7).

Lupton distinguishes a 'civilised' and a 'grotesque' body, coextensive with the distinction between mind and body, in which the civilised body is considered to be closer to culture and the grotesque body closer to nature. The civilised body is equated with conscious and rational control over the body and successful internalisation of normative rules for managing bodily processes, urges and desires. 'An unwillingness to "give in" to the desires of the flesh' means that an individual is considered to possess self-control and, consequently, to be civilised and refined (Lupton, 1995a: 8). In contrast, the grotesque body is considered unruly and undisciplined. As Lupton points out, some social groups have been considered more likely to possess a grotesque body than others. Non-whites, lower classes and women have been seen as less civilised and closer to nature, and more susceptible to and less capable of controlling sexual urges, than the post-Enlightenment ideal subject, the European white male. The female body, in nineteenth-century discourses in particular, represented the grotesque body and epitomised the danger of otherness – secret, private impulses and urges, which if unchecked might contaminate and disrupt the public space. Jane Gallop argues that the apparent absence of the body in male-dominated European thought has depended on the unacknowledged presence, elsewhere, of the bodies of other sexes, classes and races. These have functioned to 'embody the body' and to labour and care for the Master's body so that he could ignore it and 'consider himself disembodied, autonomous, and free to will' (Gallop, 1988: 20).

The gendering and sexualisation of the public/private split was an integral part of its constitution – i.e. women's exclusion from the public sphere was not 'simply a contingent historical circumstance short of the ideal', but actually 'constitutive of the very notion of the public sphere' (Thompson, 1994: 92–3).

Vision and control

Vision is connected to a discourse of control and domination in Enlightenment thinking. The use of technologies of visualisation (from the mid-nineteenth-century photography to video cameras to the computer-orientated imaging technologies of the late twentieth century) brings aspects of individual bodies and experience into view and makes them subject to knowledge and control.[4] Techniques of surveillance make private experiences public property in the name of science and rationality, as part of increasing man's control over the natural environment. Vision is highly political.

Feminist researchers have drawn attention to the dominance of visual metaphors in the production of scientific knowledge (Irigaray, 1985; Keller and Grontkowski, 1983; Love, 1991; Martin, 1990; Petchesky, 1987; Zerilli, 1991). Several authors have argued that seeing has become synonymous with knowing in Western scientific and philosophical traditions, and the eye a metaphor for mind.[5] Sight has been elevated above other senses as enabling distance between knower and known, objectifying the thing visualised. Sensory experience and relatedness as ways of knowing are debased: 'vision connects us to truth as it distances us from the corporeal' (Keller and Grontkowski, 1983: 209). It has been identified as a masculine way of knowing (Irigaray, 1985; Keller and Grontkowski, 1983). Thus, it has also been argued that seeing operates as a mode of scrutiny and surveillance in the exercise of domination and control over bodies (Foucault, 1976, 1979, 1980a), especially those of women (Irigaray, 1985; Martin, 1990; Petchesky, 1987). In particular, a *biotechnical gaze* restructures space to see the invisible, and makes the body intelligible, and controllable, on an infinitely small scale as a mosaic of detachable parts.

Scientific knowledge develops, ideally, through the collection of 'data' based on sensory perception and reflection upon these data. In conventional descriptions of scientific practice and data collection, sight is privileged above other senses (hearing, touch), which, although important, play an auxiliary role to vision. Further, vision has been regarded as the sense which places the world at the greatest distance, and which is capable of 'recording' most objectively and impartially events in the world. Thus, vision has been conventionally associated with 'disengagement' and 'objectification', signifying a relation of distance, which prioritises abstract and isolated individualism over collectivity and community.

This idealised approach to the production of knowledge prompted the early use of photography in medical and criminal records. Photography was assumed to convey immediacy and accuracy – 'the camera never lies'. Photography was used in the nineteenth century to create a typology of the sick, the insane, the criminal and any other section of the population considered 'other', and operated as a mechanism of surveillance and control (Kembler, 1995). However, Kembler points out, photography was endowed with the authority to 'tell the truth' not by 'the mechanical process of representation' but by the discourses of control and institutional contexts in which it was used (Kembler, 1995: 98).

Rosalind Petchesky (1987) has argued that ultrasonography has enabled medical experts to render women marginal to foetal development and to construct the foetus as self-made and independent. The foetus imaged in splendid isolation is represented as primary and autonomous and the woman as absent or peripheral (Petchesky, 1987: 268). This image resonates with and reinforces other dominant cultural meanings – in particular that of autonomous, disembodied non-contingent existence – which are the preconditions of reason and the rational individual. The foetus thus comes to epitomise bourgeois liberal conceptions of autonomous individualism. In a visually orientated culture, ultrasonic images of the foetus lend an existence to the foetus, which is synonymous with personhood and a public presence: foetuses are increasingly regarded as patients by physicians.

The presumption of foetal autonomy is not the inevitable outcome of technologies. Technologies take on the meanings and uses they do because of a broader cultural climate: the politics of abortion and hostility to women. Also we live in a visually orientated culture and some women may experience 'picturing the baby' as empowering, helping them to view the baby as more real and develop an attachment to it (Petchesky, 1987).[6] Women's relation to foetal imaging may also be connected with their traditional role as keepers of family albums: ultrasound images may fit within a 'familiar language of "private" images' (ibid.: 283). Foetal imaging may enhance the desired participation in, not necessarily only the appropriation of, pregnancy by partners (who may be men or women).

'Images lack "objective" meanings. Instead meanings come from "context, communication, application, and reception"' (Petchesky, 1987: 286). How pregnant women see foetal images will depend on the context of viewing, the relationship of viewer to image and what it symbolises. This might be influenced by past reproductive history (of infertility and loss, for example). Construction of the meanings of the image/visual text is an interactive process, which draws on experience and various prominent discourses (popular media provide a lens through which to see and construct the meanings of, say, family album photos and foetal images).

Some feminist and cultural theorists have argued that visualisation and objectification as privileged ways of knowing are specifically masculine (man the viewer, woman the spectacle). This may be construed as essentialist – it implies that maleness and femaleness are discrete entities and already established facts, onto which other attributes can be stitched. Alternatively, it can be argued not that 'the gaze' belongs to men, but that 'the language, perceptions and uses of visual information may be different for women, as pregnant subjects, than they are for men (or women) as physicians, researchers or reporters' (Petchesky, 1987: 275). This difference 'will reflect the historical control by men over science, medicine and obstetrics in Western society and over the historical definitions of masculinity in Western culture' (ibid.: 275–6). Petchesky argues that, whether or not 'voyeurism is a "masculinist" way of looking, the "siting" of the womb as a space to be conquered can only be had by one who stands outside it looking in' – most probably a doctor, male or female (ibid.: 276).

The womb, seemingly an interior and private space, is made visible and public though ultrasonography and, at the same time, placed under surveillance, monitored, documented and controlled. The notion of the womb as an object of power/knowledge has led to the idea that ultrasound produces a 'panoptics of the womb'.

The 'panoptic principle' was first encapsulated in plans for a new style of penitentiary (the Panopticon) in 1791,[7] and described by Foucault (1979) as a model of modern power extended to other institutions,[8] in which the Enlightenment ideals of reason and empirical observation were made to reproduce social order. Constant visibility removed all privacy and made every action public. The principle was that those under surveillance (in prison, hospital, work) could not see their supervisors and did not know whether or when they were being watched. Therefore, they had to act as though they were being watched all the time and become their own guards.[9] The major effect of the Panopticon (as a model for the operations of modern power) is to 'make it possible for a single gaze to see everything constantly', 'to induce in the inmate a state of conscious and permanent visibility that assures the automatic functioning of power' (Foucault, 1979: 173, 201). This asymmetrical gaze creates uncertainty, which produces surrender. Social control is effected through the separation, individualisation and visualisation of persons in space.[10]

On the other hand, it may be argued that medicine's new imaging technologies are liberatory, not controlling, on the grounds that they blur the boundaries between inside and outside of a woman's body, and contest their fixity in a natural world (Kembler, 1995).

Visibility and identity politics

The new social movements of the 1970s based around the unequal power relations of gender, race and sexuality sought to erode a boundary separating the public/private and invested in the distinctiveness of private and public spheres. These movements sought to draw attention to the exclusion from politics and representation of women, black people, gays and disabled people, and to create a space for them to speak of their oppressions and to articulate new political subject positions. Making 'visible' past and current oppressions and the relations of power which produced them and kept them hidden, helped to forge new identities which brought individuals into public view and made connections between personal experience and public performances.

The slogan 'The personal is the political' was promulgated by the feminist movement in the 1970s. It encapsulated the assertion that patterns of subordination and domination which prevailed in social relations were reproduced in the most intimate sphere of private life, that of sexual relations. Moreover, these relations were sustained by *social* definitions of female sexuality disguised as descriptions of 'essential' female sexuality (Weeks, 1989; Wood, 1985). The gay and lesbian movements which flourished during the same political era called on lesbians and gays to come 'out', with the implicit idea that increased collective visibility would confer greater cultural acceptability, empowerment and freedom. ('Visibility' as an issue in identity politics is discussed in the next chapter.) Visibility, in

this sense, means to exist in the space where political and economic deci-
sions are made – to count and, on a collective level, to become a force to be
reckoned with. Visibility confers a degree of power but also renders those
newly visible available to (existing) techniques of control.

Bio-power

'Bio-power' is a useful concept in thinking through relations between the
private/public, individual/social. 'Bio-power' is the term Foucault uses to
describe the processes whereby the modern state (from the eighteenth century onwards) gained access to the body, intervening in individuals'
private lives to scrutinise, monitor and control the intricacies of 'health,
modes of subsistence and habitation, living conditions, the whole space of
existence' (Foucault, 1981: 143–4). Such scrutiny generated a detailed
knowledge of the body and population and formed a key aspect of their
subjection.

In *The History of Sexuality*, Foucault discusses a transformation (starting
in the seventeenth century) of mechanisms of power operating in the West
away from the privilege of sovereign power to decide life and death
towards power over life. The 'power of death', symbolising sovereign
power, was replaced by 'the administration of bodies and the calculated
management of life' (Foucault, 1981: 140–1). Sex was privileged as 'a
means of access to both to the life of the body and the life of the species'
(ibid.: 146). Since it existed 'at the juncture of the "body" and the "population"', sex became a crucial target of a power organised around the
management of life rather than the menace of death (ibid.: 147).
Reproductive politics was a crucial aspect of the new 'life administering'
forms of power/knowledge.[11]

Foucault discusses what he calls 'four strategic unities which, beginning in the eighteenth century, formed specific mechanisms of knowledge
and power centering on sex' (Foucault, 1981: 103).[12] One of these
strategies bears directly on the reproductive female body: the 'hysterization of women's bodies'. Starting in the eighteenth century, the
'hysterization' of women's bodies, according to Foucault, comprised a
threefold processwhereby the female body was 'analyzed – qualified and
disqualified as thoroughly saturated with sexuality', defined as pathological and thereby brought under a medical gaze and subject to medical
interventions, and made responsible for the social body – bearing and
rearing children (Foucault, 1981: 104).[13] According to Foucault, the figure of
'the mother' constituted 'the most visible form of this hysterization' (ibid.).
However, Foucault's concept of bio-power needs developing to highlight
the complexities of difference, for example among subjects positioned as
mothers and women.

Bio-power is one tool for thinking about the relations between the individual body and populations, sex and societies. Contemporary examples

of the workings of bio-power are evident in 'public health discourse' and 'health promotion practices'. Prescriptions for sexual health link private acts to 'the public good'. They depend on a cultural perception of health as an ideal and the concept of 'risk' as a device for galvanising individuals into actively pursuing health as a personal goal.

The cultural importance of 'health'

'Health' appears to be equated with morality and is central to discourse on sexuality. The conflation of health with sexuality is not new. In nineteenth-century Britain and North America, fears about national decay and urban degeneration focused very much on sexuality – singling out the prostitute and the excessive procreation of the so-called *unfit* (the poor, certain ethnic groups, the mentally ill) as sources of disease and danger to public health and national strength (Gordon, 1977; Poovey, 1990; Weeks, 1989).

Moral judgments are, according to Deborah Lupton, central to the logic of public health (Lupton, 1995a: 4). So too is an emphasis on specific forms of rationality. Public health and health promotion directives impel individuals to adopt practices and 'healthy lifestyles' geared toward avoiding disease and stress the importance of (specific understandings of) 'rational action'. 'Rational action' is narrowly defined. The practices and policies of public health and health promotion, Lupton suggests, 'valorise some groups and individuals and marginalise others', and privilege some concepts of subjectivity and rationality and exclude others (Lupton, 1995a: 5).

> All are directed at constructing and normalising a certain kind of subject; a subject who is autonomous, directed at self-improvement, self-regulated, desirous of knowledge, a subject who is seeking happiness and healthiness. All depend on a limited collection of valorised knowledges and experts to support their claims. (Lupton, 1995a: 11)

Public health discourses rely on a notion of health as the absence of disease, which is viewed as something which can be predicted, anticipated and acted upon. This view rests on assumptions about the primacy of health as a goal for all, the nature of rational action and the function of information/knowledge in achieving these ends. How do individuals come to participate in self-surveillance health promotion activities? Lupton suggests that 'individuals are interpellated, or hailed, by the discourses of public health and health promotion'.[14] They may either 'recognise themselves as subjects of the discourse', or 'reject the discourse pertaining to them' (Lupton, 1995a: 5).

The construct *risk* plays a key role in motivating health promotion activities.

Sexuality and danger

Sexuality and the sexual body have become insinuated by a discourse on risk. This has achieved particular prominence and become a 'central cultural construct' in Western societies (Douglas, 1990; Lupton, 1995a). Mary Douglas (1990) writes that 'a culture needs a common forensic vocabulary with which to hold persons accountable' and, in current times, the word 'risk' serves 'the forensic needs of the new global culture' (Douglas, 1990: 1).

Douglas argues that in previous centuries *risk* was used as a 'neutral' term to denote the probability of an event occurring, including the likely scale of losses and gains entailed, and constituted 'a specialised mathematics of chance'. Risk was about quantification, measurement and calculation. Nowadays, the word means danger and refers only to negative and undesirable outcomes. It is also highly political. Douglas suggests that the term risk is used instead of danger because it has 'the aura of science' and 'the pretension of a possible precise calculation' (Douglas, 1990: 4).

'A philosophy of risk', according to Lupton, is part of a rationalist understanding of reality in which things do not happen without warning and 'unfortunate events are deemed to be both predictable and avoidable' – 'risk discourse is an attempt to tame uncertainty' (Lupton, 1995a: 79).

> The imperative to *do* something, to remove the source of a health risk, however tenuous, impels action. The discourse of risk becomes a political strategy, a way of negotiating the dialectic between private fears and public dangers. (Lupton, 1995a: 80)

As a technology, risk bears the hallmark of modernity in that it entails an attempt to predict and master the future and underlines the assumption that more detailed information and knowledge will lead self-evidently to more complete mastery of danger. Ironically, biomedical endeavours to produce more exact knowledge (and, hence, solutions) about and control of risk, including more detailed calibrations of factors constituting risks, produce more, not less, uncertainty and a plurality of actions and anxieties.

Lupton argues that, since the advent of the HIV/AIDS epidemic, a discourse of risk has colonised sexual behaviour and attempted to construct new ways of expressing sexual desire. The privileging of rationality in much scientific and public health discourse fails to take account of the role of the unconscious, desire and pleasure in sexual expression. For some, risk taking may be pleasurable, providing an escape from boring everyday existence and representing the danger of the forbidden. After all, much of 'the sexual' has been historically and culturally inscribed with a sense of danger and temptation. The discourse on safer sex assumes that pleasure and desire can be reorganised in response to imperatives based on health risk and that it is possible to construct a new body capable of taking pleasure in a new form of discipline (Lupton, 1995a: 87). Self-control is implied in safer sex. Sexuality is assumed to be contained within the individual. However, the dominant way in which people understand sexuality is, perhaps, in terms of irrationality, passion and irresistibility (Lupton, 1995a: 87–8).

Discourse on risk has focused on the sexual body and sexual behaviour: 'Definitions of risk serve to identify Self and Other, to apportion blame upon stigmatised minorities, or as a political weapon' (Lupton, 1995a: 91). Risk discourse provides a powerful rationale, cloaked in the neutral language of public health and health promotion, to stigmatise minority groups for their state of health. Public health discourse operates to identify disease in specific social groups, whereas clinical medicine locates disease in specific parts of the body (Lupton, 1995a).

One of the regulative effects of new technologies of risk is the production and normalisation of an increased cultural willingness to engage in greater self-scrutiny (Barsky, 1988: 114). Calculations of the distribution of disease risk bring about the segmentation of populations. Risk factors in populations operate as 'mechanisms of power that frame the everyday lives of individuals', placing under surveillance 'their everyday behaviours, their identity, their activity, their apparently unimportant gestures' (Foucault, 1979: 77) and distributing each body among the living, the sick and the dead. Individuals engaging in this degree of detailed self-scrutiny may become, as in Bentham's Panopticon, major participants in their own subjection (Foucault, 1979: 200; 1980a: 152).

Shifting boundaries

The private and the public are mobile and interdependent categories. Neither has meaning without the other. In contemporary societies, many of the meanings of sexuality are constituted in relation to changing definitions of public and private and a shifting border between them. Transgressions of this border help to constitute categories of sexual experience and perform a normative function, since representations of private sex made public are accompanied by an indication of whether or not they should be tolerated. Sexuality, in turn, gives meaning to and links the domains of private and public and, through this, links the individual to broader cultural and political structures in a way that makes social (dis)order possible. Sexuality is central to the power relations constituting modern societies.

New and changing technologies shape how and when public and private spaces are constituted as separate entities. Contemporary technologies of communication, from newspaper to the electronic creation of virtual communities, create multiple new public spaces which encroach upon and erode our sense of what is private. Various private and public spaces are actively created by subjects, such as ourselves, who read newspapers, watch television or surf the Internet, sifting through and selecting out information about others and actively disclosing and constructing facts about ourselves as we slip into virtual communities, identities and bodies.

Notes

1.   Increasing breastfeeding rates was one of the aims of the last Conservative Government's White Paper, *The Health of the Nation* (Department of Health, 1992) – although it has been argued that this initiative has not been financially supported.

2.   Hunt cites a 1993 survey by the Royal College of Midwives which found that 50 per cent of men object to women breastfeeding in front of them.

3.   The concept of 'resignification' (Butler, 1992a) is discussed in the next chapter.

4.   According to Kembler (1995), the differences between old and new technologies are not so great. For example, new medical imaging technologies bring to the fore a discourse of control and domination but this was institutionalised (though unstable) as early as the nineteenth century with the advent of photography.

5.   The importance of sight in the producton of knowledge is indicated by the frequency with which the terms 'seeing' and 'knowing' are used interchangeably. To say 'I see', in response to another's statements, is to say also 'I understand', and therefore to imply 'I know'. The mind and eye have become synonymous in much Western scientific and philosophical thought. The phrase 'in the mind's eye' says as much. The phrase 'the Enlightenment' refers directly to this coupling of vision and knowledge based upon understanding – the shedding of *light* upon a subject which enables one to see and know what was previously in darkness, lack of vision and unknown.

6.   Objectification, and the detachment of the viewer from the viewed, may make erotic and intellectual attachment possible – not only as a 'masculinist' activity but for a variety of women (who have access to this technology) (Petchesky, 1987).

7.   'Panopticon' refers to the plans submitted in 1791 by Jeremy Bentham (liberal philosopher and prison reformer) for a new style of penitentiary. The physical architecture of the Panopticon and the visibility it ensured were central to the way in which control was exercised over inmates. The Panopticon comprised a central tower opening onto a peripheral building divided into cells, each with two windows: one on the inside corresponding to the windows in the tower, the other on the outside. The supervisor observing from the tower would be able to see, against the backlight, the captive shapes, one in each cell. The supervisor could not *be seen*, because of a system of lighting and an arrangement of wooden blinds. Side walls prevented communication with fellow inmates. Each captive was constantly visible and alone 'he is seen, but does not see; he is the object of information, never a subject of communication' (Foucault, 1979: 200).

8.   This model prison was not actually built as such but the model of power it incorporated has, according to Foucault, been implemented in schools, hospitals and factories.

9.   The main principles of the Panopticon, facilitated by its architecture, were: an asymmetrical gaze; the isolation and solitude of prisoners; the internalisation of the gaze; the invisibility of the surveillance; its automatic character; the involvement of subjects in their own surveillance.

10. The unruly crowd is made manageable: no plots of escape from prison; no danger of contagion if they are sick; no mutual violence if they are mad; no chatter if they are children; no disorders or coalitions if they are workers (Foucault, 1979).

11. Bio-power was an indispensable element in the development of capitalism since it made possible 'a controlled insertion of bodies into the machinery of production' (Foucault, 1981: 141). Bio-power must also, as Jana Sawicki points out, have been 'indispensable to patriarchal power insofar as it provided instruments for the insertion of women's bodies into the machinery of reproduction' (Sawicki, 1991: 68).

12. Foucault argues that there is 'no single, all-encompassing strategy, valid for all of society and bearing on all the manifestations of sex' (1981: 103). According to Foucault, it is a mistake to 'reduce all of sex to its reproductive function' since this fails to take account of the many objectives and means employed in sexual politics.

13. The 'hysterization' of women's bodies, according to Foucault entailed

> a threefold process whereby the female body was analyzed – qualified and disqualified as thoroughly saturated with sexuality; whereby it was integrated into the sphere of medical practices by reason of a pathology intrinsic to it; whereby, finally, it was placed in organic communication with the social body (whose regulated fecundity it was supposed to ensure), the family space (of which it had to be a substantial and functional element), and the life of children (which it produced and had to guarantee, by virtue of a biologico-moral responsibility lasting through the entire period of the children's education): the Mother, with her negative image of 'nervous woman', constituted the most visible form of this hysterization. (Foucault, 1981: 104)

14. Louis Althusser used the term 'interpellation' to refer to a process whereby specific ideologies operate to construct subjects and make them into agents, or carriers, of social structure. Interpellation is analogous to hailing a person in the street. Ideologies operate as discourse, addressing or interpellating individuals as subjects in a certain way, thereby bestowing on them 'a particular identity or subjectivity and position in society' (Thompson, 1992: 342). There is, however, a mechanical implication in Althusser's conceptualisation of interpellation, which 'assumes that people automatically recognise themselves in terms of the categories by which they are "hailed", and it neglects the processes by which people negotiate their own identities and the various ways in which they are motivated to act in accordance with them' (Thompson, 1986: 25).

4

SEX/UALITY AND REPRESENTATION

Sex in 'the media'

Frequent public exposure of closet (homo and hetero) sexual liaisons and salacious media coverage of these suggest that contemporary western cultural horizons are crowded with different sexual possibilities. Lesbian and gay sexualities, increasingly visible in the media and popular culture, are represented as exciting and glamorous (Hamer and Budge, 1994). Stars of stage, film, television and music have 'come out' (or been 'outed') all over the place. By now, most British and several US soaps have entertained audiences with a gay or lesbian storyline, and high camp has permeated the conservative genre of costume drama.[1] Homo-erotic imagery has been successfully used to (re)package and sell a variety of consumer items. A few years ago, the media coined the term 'lesbian chic', which let the public know just how sexy and fashionable lesbianism was. One British journalist complained, at the time, that 'lesbianism' was displacing interest in vital issues like Prince Charles's love life, mad cow disease and air pollution (*Observer*, 7 July 1994).

Lesbian and gay characters in the mainstream invariably attract further media attention and comment. So, what does this mean? Has 'perversity' become acceptable and even desirable as a practice and identity? What have been the political effects of such heightened diversity and 'visibility'? Are we living in a time of radical sexual pluralism? Is this an example of 'decentred' and 'plastic' sexuality (Giddens, 1993)?

Visibility is connected with power (as discussed in Chapter 3). Media representation may confer visibility and power. For some, representation in the media *is* power (Gross, 1989). According to Larry Gross, writing in the late 1980s, 'invisibility' keeps powerless groups at the bottom of hierarchies. Gross argues that 'sexual minorities' have been excluded from mainstream representation and thereby rendered invisible. When they are represented they are negatively portrayed. Under- or negative representation means that lesbians and gays are seen as having an inferior or pathological sexuality. Gross argues that the media could potentially confer positive visibility on these groups and so liberate them from the oppression they suffer as a result of invisibility and/or negative portrayal. The trouble is, Gross argues, when groups or perspectives do attain visibility, the way in which they are represented reflects the biases and interests of those elites who define the public agenda ((mostly) white, middle-aged, male, middle and upper-class, and heterosexual). Mainstream film and TV are nearly always presented as transparent mediators of reality which can and do show us how people and places look – *the way it is*. Gays are mainly villains or victims and stories about gays are told from the perspective of a straight audience struggling to understand. According to Gross, the most effective form of resistance to the hegemonic force of the dominant media is to 'speak ourselves'.

To some extent, things seem to have changed in the 1990s. Lesbians and gays are more visible in the mainstream and are not always negatively portrayed. Lesbian and gay characters are also good looking and successful, with nice friends (who do not mind that they are queer), homes and jobs. Perhaps these images too may be viewed as narrow and 'unrepresentative'. On the other hand, (openly declared) lesbian and gay producers and film makers are working in the mainstream to produce straight programmes and, sometimes, programmes from a lesbian or gay perspective for lesbian and gay audiences. Out of the mainstream, lesbians and gays produce a range of newspapers, magazines, books, films, exhibitions and festivals for lesbian and gay audiences. It may be claimed that these forms of representation are experienced as positive and 'affirmative'.

The extent to which particular instances of visibility may be seen as positive or not and the degree to which they may confer power is a matter of debate. However, there is a more significant consideration here. The argument put forward by Gross (and others) is problematic, I suggest, because of the assumptions made about what identity is and how representation works. This argument assumes that there is a lesbian or gay sexuality which exists in advance of representation and can then be mis-represented (by under- or negative representation) or accurately represented and positively affirmed through a lesbian or gay 'perspective'. That is, representation is assumed to *describe* an existing reality, for better or worse. Even though Gross may see sexuality as socially constructed (as healthy or pathological, depending on the perspective) the identities described are *essentialised*, because they are portrayed as pre-existing facts about, or attributes of, individuals. In addition, lesbians and gays in the media and in life (producers, characters and audiences) are assumed to speak with a common voice and adopt a shared perspective which reflects a single basic 'subject position' – being lesbian/gay. This approach ignores the ways in which other categories of experience (class, gender, race, age, locality) variously intersect with the sexual to produce differently positioned subjects and huge variations in practices, interests and resources.

An alternative view holds that representation is a constructive act and constitutive of the phenomena which it appears to describe. The media are not vehicles for meanings and identities which already exist but a process through which they are produced and invented (Hall, 1990). These ideas and arguments are part of a much wider academic inquiry into identity and representation and are explored later in this chapter. I reject Gross's distinction between mainstream and alternative media of communication, visibility and invisibility, which implies that each is a unified and coherent entity, in favour of a focus on the productive and regulatory functions of all representation.

Undoubtedly, media representations of homosexuality have created a certain *frisson*. However, the political consequences of the apparent 'visibility' of lesbians and gays in the mainstream media and popular culture may have been more conservative than radical. Heterosexual romance and sex dominate, even to the extent that this may appear mundane and boring. Flirtations with homosexuality may just serve to resuscitate and revitalise somewhat overexposed and worn out representations of heterosexuality (Harding, J., 1994; Wilson, 1990).

Lesbian and gay sexualities have not only been publicly celebrated in recent times. In other public spheres, at work, on the streets and in health care settings, lesbian and gays have been subjected to insults, discrimination and 'bashings'. Also, lesbians and gays are not the only 'troublesome' sexualities in the media spotlight. Single mothers, absent fathers, adulterous public figures and those living with HIV/AIDS have been demonised for possessing aberrant sexualities. Other vilified forms of 'the sexual' include representations of violent acts like rape, child sexual abuse and pornography, incest and sex tourism. The media have also helped to shape other forms of sexuality for a public gaze and provoke debate about their legitimacy – for example, debate about *who* can and should have access to new reproductive technologies and the sexualisation of children in advertising.[2]

What are we to make of the apparent overexposure of sex, its diversity, and its prominence in the public domain? The influence of the media is not new. Gagnon and Parker argue that, by the late 1970s, the mass media in the US not only transmitted the results of sex research, but had become 'the major vehicle for the display and explanation of sexuality' (Gagnon and Parker: 1995: 7). Consequently, subsequent findings of sex research in the 1980s and 1990s 'were foregrounded against a more sexually explicit media system' (ibid.). Working from the perspective that representation is productive (not reflective) of the phenomena it appears to describe, I suggest that the media are key players in defining what the sexual comprises and inventing sexualities. This is apparent in (a) the media's 'reporting' of sex research and dissemination of some of its findings, and the selection, interpretation and inflection of these; (b) the focus on sex 'problems' and emergence of 'sexperts' (amateur sex experts engaged in giving advice through the media to individuals who identify themselves as having a problem); (c) the emergence of 'media-originated studies of sexuality' (ibid.); (d) detailed focus on documenting and bringing to public attention 'troublesome' and 'perverse' sexualities.

Media inventions of sexuality constantly press at the limits of what is permitted by regulatory bodies and 'public' attitudes – the sexual forms and practices which can be publicly displayed and acknowledged. Through the theatrics of exposing private sex acts to a public gaze, media institutions appear to make the 'individual' accountable to 'society'. In this sense, the media articulate a relation between the private and public domains, and help to constitute them as coherent and discrete (mutually exclusive) entities.

The media constitute an arena where matters of public life are played out (McQuail, 1994). They formulate sexual matters for public attention and help to define acceptable and unacceptable, normal and abnormal, versions of sexuality.[3] That is, sexuality is always represented within a context which is never neutral but which provokes particular connotations and indicates a preferred reading identifying forms of sexual contact (for example, adult/child) which are to be publicly disavowed. This is not to imply that the media are omnipotent or autonomous or monolithic. To clarify, I use *the media* to refer to the media of mass communication (newspapers, television, radio, popular cinema, especially). I work from the assumptions that the mass media are of huge and increasing significance in contemporary societies (McQuail, 1994) and that they can be viewed as social practices linked to but not reducible to other social practices (Stevenson, 1995). The significance of the mass media as objects of cultural analysis derives from the idea that they constitute a 'power resource', that is, 'a means of influence, control and innovation in society' and 'the primary means of transmission and source of information essential to the working of most institutions' (McQuail, 1994: 1). The ways in which power operates in/through the media is a matter of debate within cultural/social theory. I view the media as a collection of institutional sites and social practices through which various prevailing discourses are articulated and work to transmit power relations and, for example, impel and constrain 'gender performances'. Indeed, the problematisation of single motherhood, teenage pregnancy and absentee fathers (as examples of 'troublesome' sexuality) helps to redefine the married heterosexual couple as the normal and acceptable reproductive unit. The norms of (unproblematic) heterosexuality are reinvented through the construction and pathologisation of 'other' sexualities.

New technologies mean that the media are rapidly involving audiences in sexual matters to an unprecedented degree. The Internet, in particular, has opened up new possibilities for pornographic consumption, paedophilia, sex tourism and gender-bending, and for sex without (real) bodies – virtual sex. Nick Stevenson suggests that, in postmodernity, 'the mass media are conceptualised both as technologically interrelated and as promoting a historically unstable domain of popular intertextuality' (1995: 2).

Sexuality as spectacle clearly fascinates. It appears to comprise multiple and diverse desires. Yet, sexual forms are consistently defined in relation to the limited possibilities of sex and gender. Next, I discuss relations between sex, gender and sexuality and the possible applications of Judith Butler's 'performative theory of gender', then go on to say a bit more about representation as production.

Sex, gender and sexuality

Individuals in Western cultures are continually addressed through various discourses (medical, juridical, aesthetic) and media and popular culture as sexually desiring subjects. They are expected to have and be in control of a sexuality. Sexuality is seen as an expression of the innermost essence and truth of our existence, what we *are* naturally, and as confirmation of gendered identity.

The prevailing assumption is that this sexuality is intelligible as either heterosexual or homosexual. However, such a definition of sexuality is only possible and meaningful in the context of the prior and incontrovertible existence of gendered identity as an unambiguous duality. Crucially, it is as a man or a woman that the individual desires and, inevitably, directs that desire towards a man or a woman.

In the 1990s, the signifiers 'man' and 'woman' appear to draw together myriad possible signifieds. There are many different ways of looking, feeling, conducting oneself as a man or as a woman. However, it must be clear which category, man or woman, is being qualified by attributes or traits considered 'feminine' or 'masculine'. A masculine or butch woman is problematically but decidedly a woman. In every appearance, style and conduct, even those which muddle and confuse gender, the binary categorisation of gender is summoned and reinforced. Transgressive acts, like cross-dressing and drag, evoke and fortify a border separating masculine and feminine. Each individual is compelled to be a gender. Individuals become culturally intelligible as human beings only as they are assigned to one of two mutually exclusive categories. It is hard to address highly ambiguous individuals without endeavouring to establish which gender is being impersonated by the other. A great deal of cultural security is invested in the idea that beneath superficial variations in the appearance of gender, including sometimes misleading appearances, lies the fundamental and intransigent reality of sex. The naked truth of the anatomical body, which is coherently and consistently differentiated from an opposing signified body, unequivocally male or female, is the substratum upon which the edifice of gender is built. Gender is taken to be the interpretation of sex in culture or the way the sexed body is lived.

Medical and other cultural conventions take genital morphology to be the definitive sign of sex. Ambiguities in genitalia (hermaphroditism) are likely to be diagnosed at birth as problems to be solved, often chemically or surgically. The conviction that an individual's genitalia are in opposition to his/her gender may also be diagnosed as a problem in adulthood and eventually lead to 'sex change' surgery. Both processes reinforce a cultural commitment to a binary system of gender based on and determined by two mutually exclusive sexes fully inscribed by one of two sets of genitals. Some individuals have tried to create a space for a third sex, which is neither male nor female – for example, subjects already assigned to the category 'women' have claimed to take sex hormones (testosterone) to provoke 'masculinising' effects (growth of facial hair, deeper voices, enlarged clitorises) and some-times adopt the pronoun 'he'. Such individuals may well be stretching the bounds of cultural understandings of sex and gender, although the terms male and female remain the relevant points of reference. Interest hovers around the idea that they are moving from one to the other (and fades once they have arrived).

A distinction between sex and gender is central to a number of dis-courses. Where this is the case, sex poses as 'the real', material, corporeal base upon which 'gender operates as an act of cultural *inscription*' (Butler, 1990a: 146). Biomedical discourse has elaborated a definitive range of sex characteristics and stipulated the ways in which sexuality and physical, psychological and social attributes and conducts follow directly from a body which is already anatomically male or female. This conceptualisation of sexual difference has been used to provide a causal explanation (written on the body) for the uneven distributions of power between gendered subjects. Historically, much feminist discourse has supported this causal sequence by distinguishing gender from sex as part of the argument that gender is *culturally* constructed and is, therefore, not inevitable. Gender inequalities, if they are culturally constructed and historically specific, may be reconstructed in culture. The idea that 'gender' is a cultural con-struct, amenable to challenge and transformation, has entailed an insistence that it is *not* a direct result of male and female bodies (Butler, 1990a). Whilst this line of argument challenges the assumption that 'biol-ogy is destiny', it assumes as *given* an anatomically male or female body. The unambiguously sexed body is simply the foundation on which the edi-fice of gender is built and might be rebuilt and is not itself the object of deconstruction. The main difficulties with feminist theorising based on a sex/gender distinction are that it does not take account of the ways in which the body is 'produced' and invested in culture and the part it plays in the production, control and regulation of subjects. In contrast, a growing number of feminist theorists have criticised the 'essentialism' of this cri-tique and refused to subscribe to a sex/gender distinction (Butler, 1990a; Grosz, 1987; Grosz and Probyn, 1995; Oudshoorn, 1994; Riley, 1988). Judith Butler's critique and, in particular, her reading of Foucault is especially interesting. Butler argues with Foucault (1981) that sex is an effect, rather than a cause, of gender relations (Butler, 1990a: 7). The specific regime of contemporary heterosexuality, far from being the natural outcome of bio-logically given sex, produces sex as its (heterosexuality's) origin and imperative.

Foucault is most often credited with *inverting* relations between sex and gender and showing that sexuality is coextensive with power and the cause, not the effect, of the binary categorisation and essentialisation of sex.

Although others were already working in this area,[4] Foucault's *History of Sexuality* set a framework for recent studies of the cultural construction of sexuality by showing how sexuality is historically contingent and discursively produced and, crucially, integral to the creation, regulation and control of modern subjects. According to Foucault, sexuality is a historically specific organisation of power, discourses and bodies and a mechanism by which individuals are subjected and usefully incorporated into different rhythms of production and consumption, pleasure and pain (Butler, 1990a; Foucault, 1981).

According to Foucault, the production in discourse of the discrete and binary categorisation of sex also entails a concealment of the power relations responsible for its creation by making sex 'a cause' of 'anatomical elements, biological functions, conducts, sensations, and pleasures' which, through sex, are brought together in 'an artificial unity' (Foucault, 1981: 154). Thus, sex operates as 'a causal principle' and 'a unique signifier and as a universal signified', whereby all manner of things can be made sex specific (Foucault, 1981: 154). Sex, according to Foucault (1981), whether masculine or feminine, is the historically specific and discursive product of a diffuse regulatory economy of sexuality which heterosexualises desire and institutes the production of discrete symmetrical oppositions between *feminine* and *masculine*, where these are understood as expressive attributes of *male* and *female* and the basis for expressing desire in sexual practice. The individual is impelled to be a gender and to express this through the practices of heterosexuality as the dominant, obligatory, 'compulsory' regime of sexuality in contemporary Western societies (Butler, 1990a). Desire has to be heterosexual to support the binary categorisation of sex. Within a matrix of heterosexism, reproduction can be seen as the ultimate visible expression of being a sex and having a sexuality. Thus, the female body has been required to be 'characterised primarily in terms of its reproductive function . . . inscribed on that body as the law of its natural necessity' (Butler, 1990a: 93).

This is not to say that heterosexuality is the root cause of all manifestations of the 'sexual', nor that a primary repressed sexuality lurks somewhere awaiting liberation. It can be argued equally that a heterosexual economy is not something fixed. Rather, it constitutes a powerful and pervasive historically modified mechanism for the subjection of persons. A heterosexual economy is also liable to erosion by the practice of (disavowed) non-reproductive sexualities like homosexuality, which fractures lines of continuity between male and female bodies, masculinity and femininity, expressions of desire and the hegemony of heterosexual reproduction (Butler, 1990a: 19; Foucault, 1980b, 1981).

Similarly, Monique Wittig (1992a, 1992b) argues that the term 'woman' is produced by, expressive of, and perpetuates (through its continued use) an economy of heterosexual relations. Since sex serves the economic needs of heterosexuality, Wittig argues, a lesbian is not a woman because, in refusing heterosexuality, she is no longer defined within that opposition, which necessarily produces male and female, man and woman.

'Other' sexualities also involve the subjection of individuals. Since sexuality is coextensive with power, there is no subversive or emancipatory sexuality which could be free or outside of power relations. Instead, it is possible to extend the boundaries of what is culturally intelligible by reworking and displacing elements of convention. Thus, the 'troublesome' visibility of lesbians and gays in popular culture may work to stretch the boundaries of culturally intelligible sexuality. Similarly, Butler suggests, the gay use of the feminine pronoun 'she' works to multiply the possible sites of application of the term and to reveal 'the arbitrary relation between the signifier and the signified, and to destabilise and mobilise the sign' (Butler, 1990a: 122). This usage, Butler points out, is not a colonisation of the feminine since it is 'suspect' to assume that the feminine already belongs to women. Indeed, such an assumption would uncritically reinforce the power relations producing a chain of causality linking body, gender and women.

Foucault's analysis has led to calls for the overthrow of the category of 'sex' and its regulatory effects. However, this is a contentious point for many feminist theorists since it is not certain whether the categories 'male' and 'female' are similarly 'subjected to a monolithic notion of sex' (Butler, 1992b: 346). For others, the apparent 'functionalism' of a Foucauldian analysis may inhibit efforts to unearth the full complexities of contemporary sexualities.

Rethinking the body and sex

The idea that sex is a given (printed indelibly on the body) is tenacious, even in seemingly radical critiques.

The body has become an object of interest for a wide range of theorists, many of whom have been concerned to challenge the subordination of body to mind established within modern Western philosophical and scientific traditions. This has involved theorising the bodily roots of subjectivity and examining the regulation of cultural relations at the level of the body.[5] In a range of different feminist writings, the sexed body is assumed to be the core entity or attribute that unites women and provides a foundation for feminist theory and politics. A substantial amount of feminist writing has been concerned with representing, liberating and reclaiming 'the female body' from denigration, repression, misrepresentation and control within patriarchal culture. In these feminist discourses, the female body is 'produced' as a consistent entity prior to and supporting different interpretations or versions of the feminine. The body is viewed as the raw materiality on which culture acts, a blank surface before signification, on which meaning is heaped.

The sexed body, which is to be liberated in feminist discourse, is also in need of deconstruction (Butler, 1990a). Several feminist researchers have attempted to demonstrate the ways in which the sexed body is historically, culturally and discursively constructed (Butler, 1990a; Harding, J., 1993; Oudshoorn, 1994; Riley, 1988). Denise Riley (1988: 103) argues that anyone's body is only periodically lived or treated as sexed. It cannot be assumed that 'women's bodies are systematically and exhaustively different', or that they are 'unified in an integral otherness'. Crucially, the body is a constantly changing concept and 'the body becomes visible *as* a body' only through a particular gaze, medical, aesthetic, political or any other, as an effect of power relations. The sexed body, since it is not reliably constant, cannot provide a firm foundation for 'the complications of the thousand discourses on "women"' (Riley, 1988: 105–6).

The body becomes sexed within discourse (on heterosexuality) through which it is invested with the 'idea' of natural or essential sex (Butler, 1990a; Foucault, 1981). Sex operates as a univocal construct whereby 'bodily pleasures are not merely causally reducible to this ostensibly sex-specific essence, but they become readily interpretable as manifestations or *signs* of this sex' (Butler, 1990a: 94–5).

Butler argues that, for Foucault, 'cultural values emerge as a result of an inscription on the body', and the body is understood as a blank page, 'a materiality prior to signification and form' (Butler, 1990a: 130). Butler suggests that the body is made up of a set of flexible 'boundaries, individual and social, politically maintained and signified' (ibid.: 33) and that Foucault's theory could be further radicalised by a 'critical inquiry that traces the regulatory practices within which bodily contours are constructed' to constitute 'the body' as a discrete entity (ibid.: 133). This could result in 'a critical genealogy of the naturalisation of sex and of bodies in general' (ibid.: 147) or the detailed practices through which bodies are 'made'.[6] The point of critical investigation into how meanings and bodies are constructed, as Donna Haraway states, is not to deny them but to 'build meanings and bodies that have a chance for life' (Haraway, 1989: 580), that is, to be able to use them more creatively. Indeed, the point of deconstruction is not to discover an essence prior to and untainted by construction but to understand how numerous different reconstructions might take place.

Butler argues that 'bodies cannot be said to have a signifiable existence prior to the mark of their gender' and asks: 'to what extent does the body *come into being* in and through the mark(s) of gender?' (1990a: 8); and, to what extent are the categories 'sex' and sexual difference 'necessary features of bodily identity'? (1990a: 96). (How) is the body rendered coherent through the category 'sex'?

Butler develops a 'performative theory of gender' which I now discuss in the context of other critical inquiries into cultural identities and politics.

Identity politics

Questions about 'identity' are very much at the heart of contemporary cultural analysis. 'Identity' as a sense of self and a social category has been brought under intense scrutiny in a range of theoretical/political discourses. It is a problematic term.

Most commonly, identity has been conceptualised as governed by the principle of belonging and not belonging, inclusion and exclusion, and a logic of limits and borders. In various different ways, psychoanalytic, philosophical, cultural and feminist theorists demonstrate how the formation and preservation of identity, at a psychological and sociological level, depends upon establishing and maintaining a border between that which is inside and that which is outside, excluded and 'other'. Psychoanalytic theorists have generally described how identity is established as a result of psychical identifications and defences and, additionally, social conflicts and cultural prohibitions (Fuss, 1991: 2). Feminist (psychoanalytic) theorists have described the psychological and cultural basis of identity and, in particular, the shared gender identification and the trans-historical and trans-cultural subordination of women (Butler, 1990b). Other theorists have sought to unearth the previously 'invisible' identities, based on gender, race, sexuality and class, of those culturally positioned beyond the margins of masculine, white, heterosexual, middle-class subjecthood.

The inside/outside relation, Diana Fuss points out, is integral to meaning production and signification, since 'denotation of any term is always dependent on what is exterior to it' (1991: 1). Within this logic and the language of borders and margins, any identity must be secured, its ontological boundaries strengthened, through self-protection and defence against the encroachment of the outside. At the same time, each identity relies on the transgression of its borders in order to constitute them as such. Heterosexuality is defined 'in critical opposition to that which it is not: homosexuality' (ibid.: 1). Homosexuality is necessary to define and to defend the border constituting heterosexuality. Similarly, it is argued, the feminine operates as the other and excluded in relation to the masculine and makes possible the border constituting sexual difference. The post-colonial subject confirms the prior existence of the coloniser (ibid.: 3).

The category 'homosexual', according to Foucault, was invented and characterised in the late nineteenth century,[7] producing the homosexual as an 'identity' rather than a category of 'forbidden acts' and a 'temporary aberration' (Foucault, 1981: 43). According to Weeks, there is plenty of historical evidence to suggest that heterosexual and homosexual (and many other sexual) practices may have always existed, whereas 'clearly demarcated categories and identities of "the heterosexual" or "the homosexual"' are relatively new (Weeks, 1995: 40).

> The nineteenth-century homosexual became a personage, a past, a case history, and a childhood, in addition to being a type of life, a life form and a morphology, with an indiscreet anatomy and possibly a mysterious physiology. Nothing that went into his total composition was unaffected by his sexuality. It was everywhere in him: at the root of all his actions. (Foucault, 1981: 43)

The invention of the category 'homosexual' in turn enabled the emergence, definition and hegemony, some eleven years later, of the term 'heterosexual' (Katz, 1990). Fuss argues that the first appearance of the homosexual as a 'species' also marks the moment of the homosexual's disappearance – into the closet (Fuss, 1991: 4).

Those subjects culturally positioned as 'other' are usually also disavowed and viewed as both contaminated and contaminating. As a number of writers have shown, this notion of alterity, and the hierarchical relation between subject and other, is both integral to and produced through the generation of academic knowledge, for example in the writing of history, science, anthropology and sociology (Clifford, 1986; Losche, 1989/90).

The political impact of emancipatory struggles in recent decades has been to demonstrate how prevailing relations of power in contemporary societies produce a hegemonic relation between inside and outside through which some cultural categories or identities are formulated as such, avowed and legitimised, and others, through the process of exclusion and 'othering', are banished to a realm of non-identity, non-representation and, effectively, non-existence. For those culturally positioned as outsiders, emancipatory political discourses have enabled the articulation of a shared sense of outsider-ness as an identity in its own right and rendered culturally intelligible a diverse range of lived experiences and disadvantages.

Identity has provided a mechanism whereby groups and individuals have been able to 'speak for themselves' as disadvantaged constituencies and against the mechanisms and relations of power which have produced systematic disadvantage and disavowal. In this way, Michel Foucault claims, the emergence in nineteenth-century psychiatric, juridical and other discourses of the homosexual as a disqualified category both enabled the extension of social control over this area of 'perversity' and also enabled the formation of a 'reverse' discourse, whereby 'homosexuality began to speak on its own behalf, to demand that its legitimacy or "naturality" be acknowledged' (Foucault, 1981: 101). Similarly, it has been possible to *speak as* a black, female, old, gay, lesbian or disabled person against hegemonic structures and practices producing those devalued categories. This political strategy has relied upon a definition of identity which assumes that a fundamental sameness and shared cultural experience underlies all other superficial differences and unites similarly positioned coherent and stable subjects. This definition often includes the idea that identities are trapped in the past and invisibility, silenced or distorted in the dominant discourses of history, science and philosophy, and must now be 'excavated and brought to light, expressed and represented' (Hall, 1990: 224). In the academy, this same perspective on identity has resulted in the writing of multiple new histories (for example, of women's work, gay and lesbian lifestyles, black cinema) in order to bring into view those previously hidden from history. Recently, however, this tradition has been substantially reviewed.

A politics articulated through oppositional identity categories has been increasingly viewed by a range of cultural theorists as a risky business. One of its limitations is that it tends to reaffirm, rather than undermine, the centrality of that which it attempts to resist (Fuss, 1991). Further, when the subject of a (political) discourse is assumed to be a nominated identity category, woman, or a *type* of woman (old, black, lesbian), identity is essentialised and difference naturalised (Scott, 1992: 25). The effect of essentialising any given identity category is that it is placed outside of cultural and historical processes and rendered permanent and immutable. A growing number of theorists have problematised identity categories as part of a political critique of the subject, 'essentialism' and the authority granted to shared cultural experience. This problematisation involves a critical examination of the historical and cultural construction of categories like woman, old and black.

Whilst identity categories (based on sex, race, sexuality, class, disability, age) provide important grounds for political articulation, they tend to entail a regulation of subjects, whether they operate as 'normalising categories of oppressive structures' or as 'the rallying points for a liberatory contestation of that oppression' (Butler, 1991: 13–14). New identities are not necessarily different to old ones and are usually accompanied by demands for clarity about who and what is included. Any identity category seeks to contain and control what it claims to describe and authorise (Butler, 1990b). Denise Riley (1988) writes that the term 'women' is never used without a characterisation of that collectivity, which also involves a 'naming', positioning and hence regulation of persons thus assigned. Butler usefully points out that, within feminist political discourse, the use of the category 'women' to refer to a social group, a felt sense of self and identity in common, operates on the basis of an assumed ontological and semantic integrity which has 'serious exclusionary implications' (Butler, 1990b: 325). She argues that it is necessary to honour the diversity of the category 'women' (and the ways in which it is internally fragmented by class, race, age and sexual orientation) and insist on its definitional non-closure to avoid producing in feminist theory a female subject who 'fails to represent' the 'array of embodied beings culturally positioned as women' (ibid.). Without a critique of the subject, emancipatory discourses are bound to substantially regulate, exclude, and put outside in a political way, even as they attempt to 'liberate', some subjects.

An emphasis on the hybrid and temporary character of contemporary cultural identities constitutes a move against the limitations of essentialising identity categories and may open up new positions from which to speak. A refusal of discrete identities undermines the inside/outside rhetoric and asserts that no one is ever simply 'in' or 'out'. As Fuss says, most of us are inside and outside at the same time. Sometimes the distance between outside and inside is no distance at all. In order to insist on 'the subversive potential of the power of the marginal', we must already be comfortably entrenched on the inside and 'our place of enunciation' must be already central (Fuss, 1991: 5).

In short, recent feminist and cultural theory has led to a rethinking of identity. A single identity does not encapsulate all that an individual is. Nor is it lived all the time. Each individual may lay claim to any one of a number of identities (Riley, 1988). Borders are rarely secure and identity is always unstable and provisional (Kristeva, 1982). Identity categories are internally segmented and cultural identities intersect, are incommensurable and interdependent (Rutherford, 1990a). Cultural identities are not an *essence* but a *positioning* (Hall, 1990). Identities are 'produced' and 'invented'. The production of identity is never complete and always in process 'subject to the continuous "play" of history, culture and power' (ibid.: 225). This view, in turn, 'problematises the very authority and authenticity to which the term, 'cultural identity', lays claim' (ibid.: 222). Similarly Weeks (1995) argues that sexual identities are complex and changeable historical inventions. They are imagined in contingent circumstances.

Gender as performance

Gender identity, Butler argues convincingly, is not an attribute of an individual, but an act which must be repeatedly performed. Gender is not a state of *being* but a *doing*. Gender is an effect and exists only in its various manifestations. That is, there is 'no gender behind the expressions of gender' and gender identity is 'performatively constituted by the expressions that are said to be its results' (Butler, 1990a: 25). Gender, according to Butler, is 'the repeated stylization of the body, a set of repeated acts within a highly rigid regulatory frame that congeal over time to produce the appearance of substance, of a natural sort of being' (ibid.: 33).

Gender then is '*a corporeal style*', or, an act which is 'both intentional and performative' (Butler, 1990a: 139). Styles are never fully self-styled but have histories which limit possibilities. Gender is an act which must be repeated. This repetition constitutes both 'a reenactment and a reexperiencing of a set of meanings already socially established' and is the everyday and ritualised way in which they are legitimised. Although individuals 'enact', repetitions or performances are also public actions. Performance has a public character in so far as it is 'effected with a strategic aim of maintaining gender within its binary frame'. Crucially, this aim 'cannot be attributed to a subject, but, rather, must be understood to found and consolidate the subject' (Butler, 1990a: 139–40).

Gender is not a stable identity or place from which the subject acts, a locus of agency; it is an identity constituted in time through a stylised repetition of acts. Gender must be understood as 'the mundane way in which bodily gestures, movements, and styles of various kinds constitute the illusion of an abiding gendered self' (Butler, 1990a: 140). According to Butler, gender is a set of norms that can never be completely internalised because they are 'phantasmic' and 'impossible to embody'. The ideal of 'an abiding gendered self' is produced through repeated acts that seek to mirror the ideal ground of identity but which are sometimes discontinuous with it. The arbitrary relation between such acts of repetition – 'a failure to repeat, a de-formity, or parodic repetition' – exposes the tenuousness of abiding identity and opens up possibilities for transformations of gender (Butler, 1990a: 140–1).

If sex is 'a performatively enacted signification', Butler argues, it can also therefore 'occasion the parodic proliferation and subversive play of gendered meanings'. If sex and gender are multiple contested sites of meaning, then 'the very multiplicity of their construction holds out the possibility of a disruption of their univocal positioning'. No category, man or woman, white or black, straight or gay, is ever complete but is perpetually under construction and constitutes 'an ongoing discursive practice, it is open to invention and resignification' (Butler, 1990a: 32–3).

For Butler, the distinction between expression and performance is critical. If gender attributes are performative, rather than expressive, they 'effectively constitute the identity they are said to express or reveal'. Gender as performance means that 'there is no preexisting identity by which an act or attribute might be measured' and 'no true or false, real or distorted acts of gender'. The notion of a 'true gender identity' can then be seen 'as a regulatory fiction' or strategy, which 'conceals gender's performative character and the performative possibilities for proliferating gender configurations outside the restricting frames of masculinist domination and compulsory heterosexuality' (Butler, 1990a: 141).

The political/theoretical task advocated by Butler is to conduct 'a political geneaology of gender ontologies' which would be capable of deconstructing the 'appearance of gender into its constitutive acts and locate and account for these acts within the compulsory frames set by the various forces that police the social appearance of gender' (Butler, 1990a: 33). This might enable the creation of new gendered meanings.

Identity and representation

The idea that identity is produced within history, discourse and power prompts a rethinking of what happens in representation. The political project of representing groups marginalised in existing systems then entails an emphasis on the *invention* of identity rather than the rediscovery of an essential (previously hidden from history) identity. This approach views identity as constituted not outside, but within representation. Thus, cinema is not a sort of mirror held up to reflect what already exists, but 'a form of representation which is able to constitute us as new kinds of subjects, and thereby enable us to discover places from which to speak' (Hall, 1990: 236–7).

Stuart Hall, speaking about the relation between culture and representation, says that 'culture is about shared meaning' and that language is 'the privileged medium in which we "make sense" of things, in which meaning is produced and exchanged' (Hall, 1997: 1). Language operates as a *representational system* and is 'one of the "media" through which thoughts, ideas and feelings are represented in a culture' (ibid.). The production and circulation of meaning through language in different ways can be analysed in different areas of social practice – for example the mass media.

Again, representation is not simply a reflection of how things are in the real world, but a creation, production and regulation of the world of possibilities (which is always material, real and fictional) in which the designation 'real' is actually a mechanism for assigning privilege and the mark of authority to some statements and not others.

From this perspective, representation is not seen as a vehicle for particular ideological messages – mainstream or alternative – since this would imply that ideologies existed already outside of and before representation. Rather, representation is seen as a space in and through which various discourses are brought into play to form specific objects of interest – for example, sexualities. Again, discourse is a particularly useful concept.

A focus on 'discourse' replaces the idea that representation acts 'as a "vehicle" for transmitting ideologies in the services of maintaining/extending power relations' and, instead, conveys the idea that the act of representation *itself* is 'the very stuff of power relations' and 'shapes our relations to the world, ourselves and others' (Briggs and Cobley, 1998: 280).

The media of mass communication, in my view, do not tell people what to think, nor reflect back to them what they already know, so that they can reaffirm their identities. Mass media representations are productive and inventive of meanings, creating and disseminating impressions that form a large part of the cultural/significatory collateral available for individuals and groups to 'resignify' their subjectivities. Media representations can be seen as constituting (opening up and restricting) sexual landscapes and horizons on which we act.

Foucault's critique of the subject is implicit here. Foucault argues that the subject is *not* a unified sovereign entity that exists prior to discourse, but is constituted by power within discourse (Foucault, 1986). Butler adds that 'the subject is never fully constituted, but is subjected and produced time and again' (Butler, 1992a: 13). Since power relations do not stop producing the effects of power, the construction of the subject is never complete, and subjectivity must be repeatedly 'resignified'. The subject is 'neither a ground nor a product, but the permanent possibility of a certain resignifying process' (ibid.). Further, the power relations which produce the subject also constitute the horizons in which individuals act as an integral part of their capacities to act. Butler argues that the horizons on which we act are not an external theatre of operations, but 'a constitutive possibility of our very capacity to act' (ibid.: 10).

The rest of this book examines the intervention of sexual identities in and through various forms of representation (scientific, political, popular cultural) and the possible ramifications of these for the resignification of subjectivity. These critical and empirical investigations of sexual identity are informed and facilitated by aspects of Judith Butler's 'performative theory of gender'.

Subverting sex/ualities

Gender may performed and produced, but performances are not independent. The social appearances of gendered identity and heterosexuality are the effects of enactments repetitiously performed within specific historical and cultural circumstances. *Sex Acts* explores the ordinary and mundane ways in which bodies are stylised and enactments of sex compelled within the binary frame of heterosexuality. The next chapters focus on the ways in which (medical, political, popular cultural) discourses impel individuals to perform sex/ualities in specific ways, highlighting discontinuities between acts and possible subversions.

I use the term 'sex/uality' to refer to and problematise the culturally and historically entrenched idea that an *a priori* sex is expressed through a gender and then through a sexuality (Butler, 1991). 'Sex/uality' draws attention to the naturalisations of sex and gender which are assumed to underpin sexuality and the need for their deconstruction.

In the following chapters I investigate not only 'problematic' and culturally disavowed sexualities, but also supposedly ordinary and boring sexualities (straight sex, pregnancy) and regard investigations of sex, from whichever perspective, as representations which are productive and also *constraining*. The attention given to women's sexuality by feminist researchers and to homosexuality by lesbian and gay researchers, entails a degree of endorsement of unresearched, unscrutinised and therefore unproblematised sexualities – mainly heterosexual and masculine. However, each of these categories (masculine and feminine, heterosexual and homosexual) can be viewed as culturally and historically contingent and investigated in the empirical contexts in which it appears to define and constrain 'the sexual'.

Notes

1. For readings of some of these from different lesbian perspectives see Hamer and Budge (eds), *The Good, the Bad and the Gorgeous* (1984).

2. There is ongoing discussion in the media of whether women in their fifties and/or single women should have access to assisted conception using donated ova. This is discussed in Chapter 7.

3. McQuail also suggests that the mass media constitute 'the source of an ordered and public meaning system which provides a benchmark for what is *normal*, empirically and evaluatively' and that the source of deviations is signalled and comparisons made in terms of this public version of normality (McQuail, 1994: 1).

4.   Jeffrey Weeks points out that many academics (particularly feminist and gay and lesbian historians) had already been working in this field when Foucault's *History of Sexuality* was published in French in 1976 (Weeks, 1991).

5.   See for example, Foucault (1979, 1980a, 1981); Turner (1984, 1991); Deleuze and Guattari (1983); Diprose and Ferrel (1991); Kristeva (1982); Grosz (1987).

6.   Donna Haraway (1989a: 10) argues that 'Bodies are not born, they are made'.

7.   The actual date of this historical moment is 1870, according to Foucault (1981) and Weeks (1991), and 1869, according to Katz (1990).

5

CHEMICAL SEX AND SOCIAL CONTROL[1]

Controlling sex

Hormones signify control. The idea of bodies controlled by hormones has a huge appeal for late twentieth-century Euro-Americans obsessed with control (Vines, 1993). Hormones are seen as compelling specific actions and producing a vast repertoire of effects – femininity, masculinity, fertility, sexuality, sexual disorders, mental illness, violent behaviour – regardless of individual circumstances and specific socio-political contexts. The development of technologies to measure and adjust hormones has meant that deviant characteristics and behaviours can be 'corrected' at the level of the body, precluding a political account of events in favour of a biological explanation. In other words, hormonal explanations of behaviour and feelings are brought into play as corrective or normalising strategies, which depoliticise events.

The political significance of 'sex hormones' derives from the idea that they cause sexual difference in all its manifestations. Historically, the scientific study of sex hormones has been linked with efforts to manage and treat deviant sex/uality, typically problematised in women as the result of unbalanced hormonal impulses and drives.

Biomedical discourse can be seen as a site at which power relations are reproduced, and subjectivity and human embodiment constructed (Lupton, 1995a: 4). Specifically, biomedical discourse on sex hormones constitutes a very pervasive and powerful account of sex/uality, which delimits and constrains possible enactments of sex.

The hormonal body

Hormones are a major twentieth-century invention. They have captured the scientific and popular imagination because of their perceived power to account for and control how individuals look, feel and behave (Vines, 1993). In scientific and other discourses, *sex hormones* have been viewed as powerful determinants of sexual difference, providing a point of origin for sex and a mechanism whereby sexual difference is expressed on the body as a 'natural fact'. Sex hormones have been subject to medical manipulation and control, most notably through the use of synthetic hormones to prevent menopausal or premenstrual symptoms and pregnancy.

When they were 'discovered' in the early twentieth century, hormones were conceptualised as 'chemical messengers' which emanated from a single source (for example the gonads, thyroid or adrenal glands) and circulated in the blood to convey information necessary to activate precise effects in the body's disparate organs (Long Hall, 1973; Oudshoorn, 1990). Sex hormones were claimed to transmit signals necessary to stimulate the proper development of femininity or masculinity, including opposing and exclusive sets of discrete anatomical characteristics, conducts, sensations and pleasures (Harding, J., 1993). In effect, sex hormones were discursively constituted as embodying the *essence* of sex.

Sex hormones constructed in this way propelled and supported a hierarchy of events in which it was accepted that sex could be read from a body displaying one of two surface morphologies. This notion of sexual dualism has been thoroughly reinforced in subsequent discourse by the continued use of the terms 'male' and 'female' to describe hormones, implying that they function separately and exclusively to 'sex' subjects (despite biomedical claims that oestrogens are present and functional in both male and female bodies).[2] Indeed, the same dualistic assumptions about sex and the body are produced today by the use of the term 'oestrogen', which is coded as the stereotypical 'female sex hormone' and as the biological basis of femininity.

The 'discovery' of hormones facilitated the development of a specific new construct: *the hormonal body*, meaning the body controlled by hormones. The hormonal body has developed into a dominant mode of conceptualising the body and the biological basis of sexual difference (Oudshoorn, 1994).

Significantly, since hormones have been characterised as chemical drives and urges which compel specific effects, these effects have been seen as involuntary and, potentially, out of control. The conceptualisation of hormones as chemical entities has further meant that their effects have been seen as qualitatively determined by the quantity of hormones circulating in the blood. This conceptual framework has provided a basis for the development of technologies aimed at quantifying, measuring and adjusting these invisible causal agents. Such technologies, in turn, imply the setting of standards and methods for defining normality and abnormality in hormone levels and effects. They also rely on the idea that adjustment via treatments with hormones is possible and desirable. The chemical model of the body and sex, implied by the hormonal body, has opened up the possibility of identifying and interrogating numerous sites of sexual difference and subjecting them to measurement and adjustment (Harding, J., 1993).

The hormonal body, then, encompasses a set of related mechanisms aimed at bringing about the normalisation and regulation of the body and sex. The appeal of 'the hormonal body' in and beyond scientific discourse may lie in both its assumed capacity to provide a unique cause for multiple significations of sexual difference, since a variety of characteristics and behaviours deemed typically male or female have been attributed to sex hormones, and the idea that these may be open to manipulation with relative ease. The hormonal body is primarily conceptualised in relation to notions of *control*, encapsulating possibilities for both loss of control, through hormonal lack or excess, and (medical) interventions to (re)assert control over multiple and minute elements of life processes. The hormonal body provides a reassurance that scientific knowledge, its accumulation and application, can facilitate control over corporeality (Oudshoorn, 1994). The hormonal body is therefore a powerful construct with far-reaching implications, particularly for the sexed body, sexuality and medical practices.

Significantly, the female body, rather than the male body, has been represented in scientific and media publications, and clinical and everyday conversations, as entirely controlled by hormones. The hormonal body has provided a specific framework and language for explaining experiences (physical, psychological and social) and defining new diseases in women. It has facilitated the development of a range of medical interventions, including diagnostic tests and treatments, and highly profitable pharmaceutical products directed largely at women.[3] One of the most striking consequences of the hormonal body concept, Nelly Oudshoorn points out, is the extensive worldwide ingestion of hormonal pills, particularly hormonal contraceptives, by women, which has outstripped the deployment of any previous medical technology (Oudshoorn, 1994). Another significant consequence is the definition of menopause as a hormone deficiency disease affecting *all* women, in which reduced levels of oestrogen result in debilitating symptoms and diseases, ranging from night sweats to osteoporosis and cardiovascular disease (Harding, J., 1993). Hormone replacement therapy (HRT) has been widely, and controversially, promoted for short term use to relieve transient symptoms and, increasingly, for long term use to prevent physical and mental disease, loss of libido and sexual attractiveness. Thus, the female body has become subject to treatments directed at the moderation and regulation of menstruation, fertility and menopausal symptoms, all of which take as their reference point the reproductive potential of the female body and constitute this as its defining characteristic. In this way, the (female) hormonal body supports a determinedly dualistic conception of sex and its expression as reproductive heterosexuality.

Through the processes of definition, explanation and treatment, the female body continues to be confirmed as an entity thoroughly saturated with sexuality (Foucault, 1981) which in turn is defined as essentially reproductive and as such susceptible to a range of potential, if not actual, pathologies (Harding, J., 1993). The hormonal body has thereby been rendered self-evidently in need of regulation and control.

Several feminists have criticised hormonal explanations and treatments for aspects of women's experiences, particularly in relation to premenstrual syndrome and hormone replacement therapy (Coney, 1991; Greer,

1991; Klein, 1992; Vines, 1993; Worcester and Whately, 1992; Zita, 1988). However, within the critical domain of feminist discourse on HRT and other women's health issues, the ontology of the natural body and the category sex inscribed in medical discourse have not usually been questioned. More often, these discourses typically embrace the proposition that both unity and difference among women can be articulated in terms of their *experience* of their bodies. The female body is thereby produced as a stable entity denoting an 'integral otherness' (Riley, 1988) which underpins the category 'women' as a singular cultural positioning. This is, in part, the legacy of an historical distinction between sex and gender, in which it is argued that gender is not the result of a male or female body but is culturally constructed and therefore amenable to reconstruction within culture. As I mentioned in Chapter 4, within the logic of the sex/gender distinction, sex forms 'the real' corporeal base upon which gender is inscribed (Butler, 1990a). Thus, a universalised and naturalised version of the sexed body has been perpetuated by feminists who interrogate the cultural construction of gender but not that of anatomical differences.

Some feminists have critiqued the cultural positioning of women as typically out of control and in need of management and have argued that women's bodies have historically and *metonymically* represented a perceived need to manage more generalised forms of social and environmental disintegration and chaos (Shuttleworth, 1990; Smart, 1992; Vines, 1993). In doing this, writers have assumed the prior existence and coherence of the category 'women'. As others have pointed out, this has 'serious exclusionary implications' for the articulation of some political subject positions and is also 'normative' (Butler, 1990a: 325; Riley, 1988). Women are not all positioned in the same way either as patients or as objects of research. The category 'women' (as discussed in Chapter 4) is diverse and internally segmented (by class, race, age, sexual orientation). The implication is that differences within the category should be acknowledged. However, it is also important to recognise that any discourse, medical or feminist, which addresses 'women' as a generic category brings into being, positions and simultaneously regulates, versions of woman/women by stipulating both their constituent elements and the terms and conditions of their existence. Further, each version of woman is founded upon and made possible by the exclusion of other potential versions (Butler, 1990a; Riley, 1988).

In parallel with producing a univocal positioning of women, feminist analyses have tended to claim that aspects of scientific knowledge and medical practice are *masculinist*, thereby implying that sex is a prior condition underpinning a singular positioning for male researchers and theorists. Also, as others have argued, critiques of science as sexist, entailing the reproduction and reinforcement of hierarchical gender relations, imply mistakenly that it is possible to have a science free of gendered arrangements (Harding, S., 1986). In my view, it is necessary to show how scientific statements *produce* sex in the same discursive manoeuvres as they produce their own knowledge claims, authority and objects. It is at this level that the apparent sexualisation, naturalisation and universalisation of the hormonal body (as part of the discursive production and regulation of the sexed body) must be analysed.

Nelly Oudshoorn's book *Beyond the Natural Body* (1994) addresses many of these issues. In particular, her text contributes significantly to analyses of how 'the female body' has been historically and discursively produced; how it became overwhelmingly the object of sex hormone research and medical interventions, as a result of the specific material contexts in which research was conducted rather than an assumed coherence and motivation of 'male interests'; how scientists 'do science' and universalise and naturalise their creations; the development of a chemical model of sex, which also opened up the possibility that sex might be a relative, rather than an absolute, concept and the implications of this chemical model for (a diversity of) women and sex/ualities.

In *Beyond the Natural Body*, Nelly Oudshoorn traces the development of sex hormone research from the 1920s to the 1960s, focusing on conceptualisations of sex hormones and their mass production as drugs, in particular the contraceptive pill. She investigates how the detailed practices of sex hormone researchers contribute to discourse building and (re)constructions of the natural body and sex. She insists that scientists collectively create facts and artifacts in social contexts, consisting of networks with other social groups and differential access to research materials, which function as carriers in the transmission and consequent selection of knowledge claims (Oudshoorn, 1994: 79). Thus, her analysis is focused on the activities and relationships of different groups of researchers (laboratory scientists, clinicians (gynaecologists), pharmaceutical companies), their access to resources including research materials (like ovaries, testes, urine) and development of research tools (like blood tests and vaginal smear tests) and cultural notions about sex. All of these processes and elements, she claims, constitute the social dynamics and ingredients of discourse building and shape the collective creation of scientific facts about sex hormones, their origins and functions, and help to secure authority for some, and not other, knowledge claims. It is these very *material* factors, not simply an assumed *a priori* set of coherent 'male interests', that has made the female body the object of sex hormone research.[4]

The sexualisation of the hormonal body

Oudshoorn argues that the female body became the central focus of sex hormone research because of already existing institutional contexts, notably the gynaecological clinic (concerned with the reproductive functions of the female body), in which research materials like ovaries and urine could be collected, and clinical trials involving new drugs and diagnostic techniques could be conducted. In addition, this institutional context provided 'an organised audience' (consisting of clinicians and patients) for the marketing of the pharmaceutical products resulting from sex hormone research (Oudshoorn, 1994: 141). In contrast, there was no clinical practice focusing on reproduction in the male body, in which healthy or affected testes were removed, nor institutional context in which urine was routinely collected. It was only when male sex hormones could be produced synthetically that an increase in male sex hormone research took place (Oudshoorn, 1994: 77).

According to Oudshoorn, during the 1920s and 1930s the female body was increasingly subjected to hormonal treatments, which were applied universally for a wide array of diseases in women (from menstrual disorders to menopause, infertility and psychiatric disorders),[5] where these could be attributed to ovarian dysfunction. Diseases of older women were attributed to low levels of sex hormones during the menopause, which enabled symptoms previously not defined as illness to become the focus of medical interventions (Oudshoorn, 1994: 95). By the late 1930s, menopause was promoted as the major indication for treatment with female sex hormone therapy.

Hormonal control of reproduction did not develop as one of the therapeutic uses of sex hormones until the 1950s, although a mass market existed, because of prevailing moral and political attitudes towards contraception (Oudshoorn, 1994: 97–8). In particular, objections were raised to any drug that would interfere with menstruation, and therefore *nature* (ibid.: 120–1). According to Oudshoorn, sex hormone research was gradually reorientated towards contraception as a result of pressure from social movements (the birth control, the eugenics and the population control movements), all of which attempted to limit human reproduction via the separation of sexuality from reproduction (ibid.: 115–17). This apparent 'recontextualisation' of research was initiated by feminist birth control activists, rather than by scientists.[6]

Male sex hormones were not promoted to the same extent owing to technical problems in producing a 'pure' product and low expectations of their therapeutic value. The *male menopause* did not appear to be a legitimate subject of medical science, owing perhaps to the previously discredited claims of earlier scientists to revive sexual activity in elderly men, which had been seen as quackery and harmful to the development of the scientific standing of sex endocrinology (Long Hall, 1973; Oudshoorn, 1994). Again, there was a lack of institutional contexts in which to conduct clinical trials which, Oudshoorn argues, functioned as a major device in linking drugs to their audiences.

According to Oudshoorn, cultural and institutional factors served to demote contraception and the male menopause as legitimate medical subjects and promote the marketing of sex hormones as specific drugs for menstruation and the female menopause. These same factors 'facilitated a situation in which the hormonally constructed female body concept acquired its appearance as a universal, natural phenomenon' (Oudshoorn, 1994: 141; also 110).

The naturalisation of the hormonal body

Oudshoorn argues that scientific concepts attain the status of natural facts in a twofold process of '(re)contextualisation', involving the creation of contexts in which knowledge claims are accepted as scientific facts and in which technologies can work, and 'decontextualisation' whereby the contexts from which scientific facts and artifacts arise are concealed, so that they do appear to be universal and not to depend on any social context (Oudshoorn, 1994: 138–9). Whilst the concealment of contexts is central to the creation of universal facts, artifacts need specific contexts in which to work and technologies are constructed in specific contexts. Even if they are used more universally, they bear the cultural imprint of the context in which they were produced.

The processes of decontextualisation and (re)contextualisation were particularly evident in the development and clinical trial of hormonal contraception by an industrialised Western country (the US) in so-called 'underdeveloped' Caribbean countries, with the aim of producing a new *universal* contraceptive for use by women of any colour, class or educational background (Oudshoorn, 1994: 133). Implicit in this activity was the assumption that, at the level of the body, women are basically all the same and share common physical processes. Scientists emphasised similarities between women and, indeed, helped to create some of these through prescribing how to use the hormonal contraceptive pill. As Oudshoorn points out, prescriptions for use of the pill could have produced menstrual cycles of any desired length, but scientists created a 'normal' menstrual cycle of 28 days that became materialised in the pill. Since pill users have a regular four-week cycle, the pill diminishes differences and produces similarities in menstrual patterns (Oudshoorn, 1994: 137). Thus, it seems, birth control ideologies were conflated with cultural imperialism to help produce a version of the *generic* hormonally controlled female body, a universal entity, common to all women.

Whilst Oudshoorn (1994: 136) does make the point that women do not occupy 'the same position as 'objects' of scientific inquiry' and that the preoccupation with the category 'women' in feminism tends to obscure differences among women's experiences and characteristics in different cultural settings, a detailed exploration of the different positionings of gendered subjects in and beyond clinical and experimental contexts is beyond the scope of her text.

A chemical model of sex – sexual dualism and multiplicity

The most startling and revolutionary aspect of the invention of the hormonal body was perhaps its incorporation of a chemical model of sex and the body based on the idea that the essences of femininity and masculinity were located in a chemical substance, rather than, as had previously been thought, a specific organ (testis or ovary).

According to Oudshoorn, between 1905 and 1920, sex hormones were seen as sex specific in origin and function and it was thought that there were just two sex hormones, one per sex (Oudshoorn, 1994). The idea that sex hormones were chemical messengers emanating from the testes or ovaries, as the seats of masculinity or femininity respectively, gave rise to the notion that these were mutually exclusive entities. This fitted in with the dominant cultural view that women's sphere and activities were distinct from and opposed to men's (in parallel with home/work, private/public distinctions). The notion of opposition and duality was reinforced by the idea that sex hormones were fundamentally antagonistic.

Oudshoorn states that debate around the dualistic assumptions about sex hormones developed in the 1920s, intensifying when 'the female sex hormone' was found not only in the testis but also in the urine of normal, healthy men. A reconceptualisation of the *origin* of sex hormones ensued in which the categories male and female were no longer seen as mutually exclusive, rather they were combined into one sex (Oudshoorn, 1994: 28). Similarly, the idea that female sex hormones in men were dysfunctional (causing sexual and psychological disorders) gave way to the idea in the late 1930s that 'heterosexual hormones' have a function in the normal development of male organisms. In the late 1930s, the hypothesis of endocrine feedback (between the gonads and the brain) was accepted as a theory to explain interrelations between male and female sex hormones, thereby including the brain in conceptualisations of sexual development.

Sex came to be viewed as an entity without a fixed location in the body, since it was a chemical agent transported by the blood and could wander around throughout the whole body. Sex hormones were to be seen not only as substances which could affect anatomical/sexual characteristics but as 'substances that could generate manifold synergistic actions in both the male and female body'. In short, by 'attaching sex to chemicals rather than organs' scientists defined sex as 'an entity with multidirectional capacities' (Oudshoorn, 1994: 144, 34, 146).

The introduction of a chemical model of sex involved a shift away from an anatomical perspective, describing sexual characteristics, to one focused on experimentation directed at uncovering 'the causal mechanisms that control sexual differentiation'. The idea that sex is located in chemical substances implies that 'sex is an entity that can be identified and isolated from the organism' and that 'there can be too much or too little of these substances in the organism'. This in turn renders sex available in principle to measurement, quantification and manipulation (Oudshoorn, 1994: 145).

A relative and quantitative model of sex differences meant that 'all organisms can have feminine as well as masculine characteristics' and implied that 'men and women differ only in the relative amounts of their sex hormones' (Oudshoorn, 1994: 146). This opened up the possibility that an individual could be classified in many categories from 'a virile to effeminate man' or from 'a masculine to feminine female' (ibid.: 38–9). Sex could be classified in terms of male/masculine and female/feminine. Within this framework, 'an anatomical male could possess female characteristics controlled by female sex hormones, while an anatomical female could have masculine characteristics regulated by male sex hormones' (ibid.: 39). Tests for measuring hormone levels present in the blood provided tools to specify this quantitative theory by establishing the degree of femininity and masculinity in the human body. Sex endocrinologists claimed to possess a scientific test to measure the 'biological markers' of homosexuality (ibid.: 58). In a paradigm in which sex hormones were agents of masculinity and femininity, they were also thought to constitute treatments for homosexuality. This paradigm was used for the diagnosis and treatment of homosexual men (who were considered more or less feminine as a result of levels of female sex hormones acting as the agents of femininity) in the 1930s and 1940s. Here, Oudshoorn's analysis could be further developed to include a detailed examination of the role of research on and treatments of homosexuality in re-inscribing (reproductive) heterosexuality as *the* natural sexuality and expression of sexual duality.

A chemical and quantitative model of sex differences also gave rise to the notion that hormonal production followed rhythmic patterns which differed in the male and female body, the male body being characterised by its 'stable hormonal regulation' and the female body by its 'cyclic hormonal regulation'. Oudshoorn states that this led to sex differences being conceptualised in terms of 'cyclicity versus stability', accompanied by negative and positive connotations respectively. The idea of cyclicity was not new in itself, although its use as 'a basic model for understanding the specific nature of the physical features of the female body' did represent a new departure. Cyclicity was linked with a chemical substance, which regulated 'the development of a wider variety of functions than just reproductive functions' (Oudshoorn, 1994: 146–7). Cyclicity became synonymous with instability and provided the grounds for medical intervention to regulate the female body. Blood tests for measuring hormonal levels became one very important means by which the new science of sex endocrinology established its material authority over the study of sex (ibid.: 61).

A quantitative and relativist conception of sexual differences opened the way for a variety of techniques (diagnostic and therapeutic) aimed at direct and active medical interventions, especially in the lives of women and homosexuals (both of which groups could be defined in terms of endocrine imbalances). However, as Oudshoorn observes, sex endocrinologists failed to take up the *real* challenge provided by the chemical model of sex, namely, to abandon dualist assumptions about sex (Oudshoorn, 1994: 146). Instead, sex endocrinology adhered to the traditional gender classification system.

Reinventions of sex and biomedical constraints

Feminist critiques of biomedical and other technologies have tended to focus on their hazardous effects, often taking an anti-medicalisation or technophobic position, and have not interrogated the categories 'sex' and 'the body'. However, the production of specific versions of the sexed body and its naturalisation (as a support for various manifestations of sexual difference and enactments of sex/uality) can be seen as some of the most profound and political 'effects' of discourse on sex hormones. This highly political process, I suggest, has consequences for the 'sexing' of all subjects (by stipulating some of the terms and conditions of *being a sex*).

Nelly Oudshoorn's text presents a refreshingly thorough and detailed analysis of 'the making of sex hormones', showing how 'the down-to-earth activities of scientists' (such as collecting urine and ovaries) contribute to changing the meanings and practices associated with male and female bodies. She demonstrates how the female body emerged as the object of biomedical research and treatments within, and because of, existing highly gendered institutional contexts, which in turn has helped to shape constructions of sex and the body. Significantly, she highlights the persistence of dualistic assumptions about sex, despite the definition of hormones as chemical substances which supports an interpretation of biological sex as a relative and multi-directional entity.

(How) has sexual multiplicity been so effectively denied in and beyond scientific discourse? Oudshoorn suggests that the possibilities of sexual diversity have been constrained by a discourse on gender, which constructs men and women as discrete and oppositional social categories. This proposition, and the idea that women are not all similarly positioned, can and must be further developed beyond Oudshoorn's text with reference to current 1990s discourse on sex hormones.

Oudshoorn's study might be complemented by an exploration of the subjective positioning(s) of 'configurated users' of sex hormones. This might open up the otherwise silent and passive space of 'patient' to reveal how differently positioned subjects make sense of and use scientific facts and artifacts in the construction, (re)invention and enactment of sex/ualities. This enterprise might be assisted by several well known arguments (also mentioned in the previous chapter). The first is the argument that subjects of discourse are constructed within power relations (Foucault, 1986). The second argument is that, since power relations do not stop producing the effects of power, the construction of the subject is never complete, and subjectivity must be repeatedly 'resignified' (Butler, 1992a: 13). *Being a sex* is an incomplete subjective identification which must be continually and repeatedly invented and performed within a play of power, discourses and history (Butler, 1990a; Foucault, 1986; Hall, 1990, 1992; Riley, 1988; Rutherford, 1990a).

It is likely that the biomedical sciences, in particular, form part of the significatory collateral available for reinventing sex. Biomedicine provides an authoritative and pervasive framework underpinning cultural understandings of the body, which thoroughly insinuates other discourses. Unfortunately, those (feminist) philosophers who have contributed to a critical genealogy of sex and the body have not always paid sufficient attention to the impact of biomedical discourses and technologies. However, debates over the benefits and hazards of sex hormone treatments also actively participate in the production and regulation of the 'normal' sexed body as a natural and biological (therefore immutable) basis for sexual identities. Discourse on sex hormones may operate to reinscribe the sexed body as a firm foundation for the architecture of sexual difference.

An analysis of discourses on sex hormones provides an opportunity to interrogate some of the detailed practices through which bodies are 'made' and regulated, and may operate as 'an anchor for significations of gender' (Butler, 1990a), in order to see how they might be otherwise reconstructed. If sex and gender are, as Butler argues, multiple sites of contested meaning and *acts* which much be repeatedly performed, rather than attributes of individuals, then it is very important to recognise that performances are neither arbitrary nor entirely elective. Rather, they are variously constrained within existing discourses and possibilities for reworking these. In this way, the meanings of sex are not simply imposed on individuals from outside but must be actively elaborated and produced. An analysis of discourses on oestrogens provides an opportunity for examining some of the powerful cultural, historical and political factors compelling and constraining enactments of sexed identity and contestations of sexed meanings.

In Oudshoorn's text, sex is deployed in what appears to be an inevitably ambiguous way. The terms 'male' and 'female' operate both as objects to be deconstructed and as organising principles in her analysis. Ironically, this is consistent with the ambiguous positioning of sex hormones in biomedical discourse where the hormonally determined body is both already sexed and in the process of becoming sexed. Sex hormones appear capable of continually conferring sex on the body only by virtue of the fact that sex is assumed to already exist as a dichotomous and unambiguous category. 'Sex' already exists as a discursive entity to categorise both hormones and significations of the body. In this way, the hormonal body incorporates the ideas that sex is fixed yet flexible and, above all, amenable to control.

I now wish to return to the ideas that hormonal explanations of behaviour and feelings are brought into play as corrective or normalising strategies, which depoliticise events, and that, historically, the scientific study of sex hormones has been linked with efforts to manage and treat deviant sex/uality.

In the rest of this chapter I examine some of the ways in which high profile contemporary discourses on HRT compel and constrain possible enactments of sex.

Sex/uality, ageing and oestrogen replacement

Early sex hormone research (from the 1920s onwards) set the stage for the deployment of hormone replacement therapy (HRT) in the 1990s. Sex hormones were characterised in 1920s biomedical discourse as omnipotent forces which exercised a determining influence over the female body and sexuality. The power of sex hormones to anchor clusters of signification in turn has intensified the capacity of HRT to calibrate, adjust and finely tune the specific constituents of sex/uality.

Biomedical discourse of the 1920s constructed sex/uality as hormonally driven and unstable, and in need of stabilisation and control. This opened the way to infinite possibilities for adjustment through a technology of replacement. The precedent was fixed, whereby the medically constructed instabilities of feminised objects formed the basis for repeated performances of sex. Through biomedical discourse, sex achieved momentary stabilisation as a condition of its (sex's) generic instability.

The quality and quantity of sex hormones were seen to govern the normal, or abnormal, development of the body and the expression of sex/uality, considered to be synonymous with procreation. Abnormalities resulted from an excess or deficit of hormonal secretion. Medical texts at the time problematised the effects of hormonal insufficiency or excess in women – bleeding disorders, frigidity, nymphomania, homosexuality (Harding, J., 1993). Sexual ambiguity, personified in the hermaphrodite, was seen to result from inadequate hormonal influence (Frank, 1922). In this way, sex hormones were constructed as both omnipotent and requiring careful control. The possibility of measuring and adjusting hormonal levels in the body provided a ground for infinite medical interventions to moderate a range of designated abnormalities.

Discourses on HRT operate to constrain and regulate the meanings of sex/uality. They effectively inscribe a bodily basis for sex and produce a means of regulating it (by constructing it as an effect of internal chemically driven forces susceptible to adjustment).

Sexual ambiguities

Oestrogen replacement therapy has been controversial since the 1960s when Robert Wilson vigorously promoted it for all women 'from menopause to the grave' and published his book *Feminine Forever* (1966), outlining the *de-feminising* effects of oestrogen deficiency, in which he listed 26 symptoms of menopause among which sexuality and mental state figured prominently.

Wilson has achieved a degree of notoriety for his 'sexist' emphasis on the use of oestrogen replacement therapy to ensure that menopausal women do not become frigid and remain sexually attractive and available (Vines, 1993). Writing in the early 1970s, Wilson claimed that oestrogen treatment of older women would not only protect against thinning of bones, and thus help to prevent fractures, it would inhibit the development of 'ugly body contours' and ensure that 'breasts and genital organs will not shrivel', so that women undergoing treatment would be 'more pleasant to live with and would not become dull and unattractive' (Wilson and Wilson, 1972). Wilson argued that women must have sufficient oestrogen levels through their lives, until death, to ensure that they *remain feminine*. Wilson's claims construct femininity as biologically determined and subject to a masculine heterosexualising gaze and HRT as the technology necessary to maintain and reinforce sexual difference.

The idea that menopause is a disease of deficiency amenable to hormonal cure persists in medical discourse and continues to be widely publicised in the popular press. Similarly, the consequences of oestrogen deficiency continue to be represented in term of its risks to femininity and sexual attractiveness.

Journalists may be pandering to perceived popular fantasies about the capacities of technology to manipulate nature and borders separating life and death, by preserving youth and vigour (Vines, 1993). Discussion of the remedial scope of HRT resonates with other contemporary discourses on health, fitness and sexual prowess, body management and sexuality. The idea that oestrogen deficiency may leave older women sexually ambiguous might also stir interest, especially since well known public figures have 'come out' over it. Feminist writer and media star Germaine Greer and conservative MP Theresa Gorman, have 'come out' as powerful and energetic 'postmenopausal' women and have vociferously articulated diametrically opposed views on the use of HRT. Journalists have speculated on whether HRT is used by other forceful public figures like Margaret Thatcher, thereby providing a fascinating focus for a public discussion about sex/uality and power.

On one level, debate about HRT helps to stimulate consumer demand for information, services and remedies, of various kinds. On another level, talk of HRT signals a new search for old identities. Discourses on hormone replacement therapy encourage and facilitate the reshaping and invention of gendered identities and effectively inscribe them on a female body. This potentially affects all subjects through different modes of discursive inclusion and exclusion.

Sex and disease[7]

Hormone replacement therapy has attracted public attention as a technology claimed to slow down the natural degeneration and 'defeminisation' of the ageing female body. It is a medically prescribed treatment which is designed to remedy the pathological effects of oestrogen deficiency occurring at, and defining, the onset of menopause and subsequent post-menopause. HRT, it is claimed, is capable of preventing physical and mental disease, loss of libido and sexual attractiveness resulting from reduced levels of natural oestrogen in older women's bodies (Gorman and Whitehead, 1989). Since oestrogen is commonly represented as the stereotypical female sex hormone and the biological basis of femininity, the widespread promotion of HRT has come to signal, in a broader cultural context, an attempt to maintain and reinforce sexual difference.

Sex hormones, especially female sex hormones, have achieved a more global and popular significance, beyond medical discourse, as all-powerful masters of mood, sexuality, appearance and behaviour. Recently, medical experts have claimed that the prescription of HRT should be routine and long term on the grounds that oestrogen replacement affords post-menopausal women protection against the risks of developing serious debilitating and potentially fatal diseases like cardiovascular disease and osteoporosis (Law et al., 1991; MacLennan, A., 1992; Stampfer et al., 1991; Wren, 1992).[8] This claim has led medical experts to advise women to seek prolonged treatment for longterm disease and transient symptoms from menopause until death (Goldman and Tosteson, 1991; Lancet, 1991; MacLennan, A., 1991; Moon, 1991). One consequence of such advice is that huge new markets of consumers requiring both pharmaceuticals and screening services (to detect possible adverse effects accompanying this treatment) are potentially opened up. Another consequence is that significant areas of women's bodily experiences are progressively subjected to techniques of medical surveillance.

Medical claims that menopause constitutes a disease requiring treatment and that HRT may prevent growing decrepitude and sexual redundancy have been widely promulgated through various media channels. However, HRT has not met with unbridled enthusiasm. Since its first vigorous promotion in the 1960s, it has been considered controversial and its efficacy and safety have been consistently challenged. Against the therapeutic claims made for HRT, it has been argued that its effectiveness as a prophylactic has not been adequately proven (Klein, 1992; Worcester and Whately, 1992). Some have cautioned about the potential dangers to women of a new technology of 'unproven' safety and benefit, in the light of the tragic consequences of previous medical interventions like the use of DES and Thalidomide in pregnancy (Klein, 1992: 28; Worcester and Whately, 1992: 23). It has also been argued that use of HRT may be associated with an increased incidence of other diseases like breast and endometrial cancers (Coney, 1991) and that, therefore, the risks of taking HRT exceed the risks of not taking it. Further, it is claimed that it is sexist to assume, as Robert Wilson (1966) first did, that menopause results in defeminisation unless women are treated with synthetic hormones (Greer, 1991; Vines, 1993). These arguments have been made largely by feminists writing on women's health issues who have attributed the successful deployment of HRT to the 'medicalisation' of the menopause (thereby defining a normal life process as a disease needing treatment) and the commercial exploitation of fear within a contemporary Western cultural matrix of sexism and ageism (Coney, 1991; Klein, 1992; Worcester and Whately, 1992). Feminists have argued that, as an alternative and preferable means of preventing disease, women should be better informed about 'the normal healthy workings' of their bodies and choices and encouraged to adopt healthy lifestyles (Worcester and Whately, 1992).

Regardless of the actual number of women who swallow, affix or apply it, the deployment of HRT defines menopause as a nodal point in women's lives and constitutes *all* women as a coherent potential treatment group based on their common reproductive processes. It marks post-menopause as a uniform time of ageing, stretching between menopause and death, differentiated from pre-menopause by specific symptoms and disease. Importantly, it emphasises the ideas that hormones are measurable and adjustable chemical indicators of sex (Harding, J., 1993; Oudshoorn, 1994) and that sex hormones are responsible for distinguishing female from male, disease from health, infertile from fertile, desired from desiring (Harding, J., 1993).

The deployment of HRT in response to medically diagnosed oestrogen deficiency underlines the idea that there is something basically missing in the female body. Further, since the idea still lingers, from early twentieth-century medical discourse, that hormones are chemical messengers whose function is to transmit the appropriate details of femininity and masculinity, the semantics of oestrogen deficit and replacement place femininity in question. Femininity is rendered precarious, provisional and in need of reinforcement. Indeed, HRT is fast becoming a significant 'technology of power' (Foucault, 1979: 30; 1981: 12) thanks to medical claims that HRT is capable of remedying an ever-growing list of defects attributable to oestrogen deficiency and seen as undermining femininity.

Discourse on HRT centres on a range of symptoms and diseases (related to menopause and post-menopause) which operate as 'secondary sex characteristics' and expressions of an original female body. In this way, discourse on HRT participates in producing and sexing the natural body. HRT marks a crossroads in contemporary discourse on sex, which is focused almost exclusively on the post-menopausal woman.

HRT has become the focus of vigorous and pervasive debate to the extent that Renate Klein argues that for 'most women' now facing middle age, the question of whether or not to take HRT is becoming one of 'paramount importance' (Klein, 1992: 25). Debate is largely focused on the risks of using or not using HRT. Different experts and commentators, medical and feminist, have endeavoured to establish a convincing computation of the relative risks and benefits of this treatment. Each group seeks to inform women of their 'options'. All actively contribute to an 'epidemic of signification' (Treichler, 1987) and information generation which constitutes as its target a subject, the post-menopausal woman, whose existence is becoming ever more ambiguous as it hovers on the borders of normality/pathology and celebration/erasure. Each commentator encourages the postmenopausal woman to engage in practices of self-surveillance and presumes that she is willing to do so. Each presumes that health is a paramount cultural value and an ideal readily pursued by all women.

Discourses on HRT focus on the 'realities' and 'myths' of sex-linked disease as a result of menopause. In both medical and feminist discourses, menopause and post-menopause are constituted as sites for the configuration of diseases and symptoms linked with, and expressive of, sex. However, symptoms and diseases, including those claimed to be the result of fluctuations in levels of sex hormones, are not at home in a body that is already sexed. Rather, they are vital elements in producing the discursive arrangement of bodies as either male or female.

Sexual limitations in discourses on HRT

Within the critical domain of feminist discourse on women's health issues, the ontology of the natural body and the category sex inscribed in medical discourse have not been questioned. Rather than being radically different, medical and feminist discourses on HRT share several common assumptions. To begin with, both presuppose the reality of an underlying physiological body and its reproductive capacity, although they appear to interpret and invest it differently. Both medical and feminist constructions of a post-menopausal woman presuppose 'sex' as a fixed and permanent category and precondition for designating menopause and individuals requiring/not requiring treatment. In different ways, each discourse produces and depends upon the separation of a coherent and stable pre-existing female body from a more flexible and tentative femininity. Femininity is made available to modification through either biomedical interventions or resocialisation/emancipation. The female body, despite its being the malleable object of various transforming disciplinary practices (surgical, medical, cosmetic, dietary), and the site of their acceptance or rejection, is produced as the singular and intransigent site of both the biological determination and cultural construction of femininity and women, whereby it is assigned normal attributes and gains a certain visibility. Both medical and feminist discourses on HRT appear to position the female body as a constant substratum underpinning different (medicalised/unmedicalised) constructions of femininity and women.

The female body is rendered a universal fact by virtue of being seen to be outside of, and prior to, history and culture. A universalised and naturalised version of the sexed body has been produced and perpetuated through medical discourse. This version of the body has also been maintained by feminists who demonstrate that gender is culturally constructed but do not also interrogate the ways in which the body is invested in culture and, in particular, do not examine the construction of anatomical differences upon which gender relations are built.

Feminist critics call for better research and the availability to women of relevant information about the *real* risks of using HRT, alternative non-pharmaceutical therapies (for example healthy lifestyles) and knowledge about the 'normal workings' of their bodies (Coney, 1991; Worcester and Whately, 1992). Without such information, it is argued, women are *disempowered*. Thus, the female body is typically positioned as a consistent and reliable site of oppression and liberation based on acquisition of (medical) knowledge of it.

Feminist women's health strategies on HRT lack sufficient critical edge to adequately challenge and transform the regulatory effects of medical discourse. Their health discourse is stymied by persistent assumptions about the stability of a female body, and its capacity to designate an integral otherness uniting 'women' (Riley, 1988: 105), and by the continuing use of medical idiom and commitment to medically led research (National Women's Health Network, 1989; Worcester and Whately, 1992). Most texts fail to articulate clearly what they mean by 'healthy' and fail to recognise the regulatory effects of their attempts to normalise and naturalise menopause and extend and individualise consumer choices in health care. Women's health discourse needs to disengage from dominating discourses and to examine the local practices of power operating through medically nominated categories, like risk factors and disease labels, if it is to further transform relations of power.

Through their deployment of the construct 'risk', which fuels desire for health and disease prevention, medical and women's health discourses encourage women to make themselves objects of self-surveillance. The ageing woman's desire is circumscribed by a responsibility to resist her own decrepitude. This responsibility separates the vigilant from the non-vigilant, healthy and sick.

HRT can be viewed as a technology of power directed at bodies which establishes, at the level of the body, unequal distributions of power and thereby contributes to the manufacture of sexed subjects and the definition of the conditions of being a sex. Sex can be seen as an effect of the investments in the body made possible by discourses, in this case on HRT, producing its natural and normal precondition and subsequent secondary characterisations.

In this sense, discourses on sex hormones and HRT work to compel and constrain specific enactments of sex/uality. 'Sex as performance' enables *both* the regulatory scope of discourses focusing on sex, which inevitably also include characterisations of the terms and conditions of its being deemed normal and appropriate, *and* the enormous potential for resisting and subverting these.

Control, central to the concept of hormones, is differently conceived in relation to subjects differently positioned as 'men' and 'women'. Whilst women are controlled by their hormones and potentially always out of control as subjects because of them, these hormones are available to scientific control. Where environmental oestrogens are concerned men are positioned as relatively powerless and scientists as unable to manipulate these hormones. In the next chapter, I examine recent debate in the media about the effects on masculine sexuality of environmental oestrogens.

Notes

1. Sections of this chapter have been published as a review article entitled 'Sex and control: the hormonal body', *Body and Society*, 2, 1: 99–111 (Harding, J., 1996).

2. Oestrogens are said to perform 'a variety of functions related to cell growth and development' in both male and female bodies (Vines, 1993: 8).

3. Tests include: blood tests to measure levels of female and male sex shormones, the pregnancy test and vaginal smear test to detect and diagnose (possibly malignant) cervical changes. Pharmaceutical products include hormonal contraceptives, hormone replacement therapy for menopause symptoms and disease prevention, and treatments for premenstrual syndrome.

4. Oudshoorn suggests that the notion of male interests implies that they are already 'given' rather than collectively created and shaped together with 'technology-in-the-making' (Oudshoorn, 1994).

5. According to Oudshoorn, medical indications for hormonal therapy were considerably expanded in connection with clinical trials during the 1920s and early 1930s. These ranged from treatment of menstrual disorders (particularly amenorrhoea) to the treatment of menopause, infertility, and problems of genital organs. By 1927, trials were extended to female psychiatric patients for treatment of schizophrenia and melancholia and then for psychoses and depression where these were attributed to disorders in the menstrual cycle. In 1929, use of female sex hormone therapy was extended to dermatological diseases (such as eczema) and diseases of the joints, where these disorders were considered to be related to ovarian dysfunction (Oudshoorn, 1994: 93).

6. Margaret Sanger, in particular, helped to make it a research issue and provide funds (Oudshoorn, 1994).

7. Parts of the rest of this chapter also appear in 'Regulating sex: constructions of the postmenopausal woman in discourses on hormone replacement therapy' (Harding, J., 1993) and 'Bodies at risk' (Harding, J., 1997).

8. The authors of several recent editorials in major medical publications claim that coronary heart disease ranks as 'number one in the causes of major disability in later life' (MacLennan, A., 1991) and 'the most common cause of death in women' (Goldman and Tosteson, 1991: 800); osteoporosis constitutes 'a major cause of morbidity in women' and that menopausal symptomatology is 'a leading cause of discomfort in women' (ibid.). For reference to osteoporosis and cardiovascular disease as disabling and life threatening, see also Law et al., 1991; Stampfer et al., 1991; Wren, 1992.

6

'GENDER-BENDING' AND MASCULINITY

'Gender-bending pollution' – a matter of public concern

Recently, public attention has been focused on an all-pervasive threat to male sex/uality. *Environmental oestrogens*, dubbed the 'gender-bending chemicals', are said to be *everywhere* in the environment and slowly and invisibly 'demasculinising' men.

A critical inquiry into sex/ualities needs to deconstruct the discursive mechanisms whereby gender is produced as a coherent and consistent entity, in order to create possibilities for ongoing reconstructions of gender. Such inquiry must interrogate sex and the body to reveal the ways in which they have been 'naturalised' and produced as anchors for significa-tions of gender (Butler, 1990a). In the previous chapter I analysed some of the ways in which the female body is discursively produced and natu-ralised. Here, for reasons I later elaborate, I intend to focus on the production of male bodies and masculinity. I am interested in how and when men become variously embodied and the body is constituted as male. This chapter explores some local sites where the male heterosexual body is organised and represented – that is, produced and invented. It examines recently publicised concerns about the adverse effects on the male body of environmental oestrogens and explores their implications for theorising gendered embodiment and identity.

Recently, the Institute for Environment and Health (IEH) published a report on the consequences to human health and wildlife of environmental oestrogens (IEH, 1995). This report appeared to trigger a sense of gendered alarm, articulated most vociferously by environmentalists and journalists. There were calls for 'urgent action' against this '"gender bending" pollu-tion' (*Guardian*, 25 July 1995). Both the report and responses to it underlined concerns about the scope of possible threats posed by envi-ronmental oestrogens to both the foetal and adult male body, its reproductive capacity and masculinity, via a process of 'feminisation'. In summer 1996, the so-called 'infant formula scare' centred on the claim that the presence of 'gender-bending chemicals' in infant feeds might damage the sexual organs of male babies and reduce their fertility as adults and, so, 'demasculinise' them. The 'normal heterosexual male body', it seemed, was becoming an (increasingly problematic) object of public interest.

Here, I examine scientific discourse as it is promulgated through the press. I analyse newspaper coverage of debate about the effects of environmental oestrogens in drinking water, foodstuffs and other products.[1] I analyse the deployment of the term 'gender-bending chemicals' and discuss how and when males may be in danger of 'feminisation' or 'demasculinisation'. I am concerned to reveal the ways in which the body is configured and invested by discourse on environmental oestrogens.

Again, I emphasise the organising and productive functions of discourse (Foucault, 1986). That is, I look at how bodies are produced, arranged, organised as sexed in and through discourse. Science is treated as one of a number of possible discourses, which is historically and culturally situated, in order to delegitimise the considerable 'authority' it appears to command (this point is discussed further in Chapter 2). My aim is to reveal some of the cultural meanings underpinning scientific statements.

I am interested in media coverage of the findings of scientific research because journalists bring scientific statements into a public arena and make them a focus of interest – that is, *popularise* them. Through a process of popularisation, selected scientific statements are made available for use in the production of cultural understandings of the body (at a public and personal level). Indeed, biomedical science has come to dominate twentieth-century discourse on the body to such an extent that scientific statements promulgated by the mass media as news and entertainment compel the everyday understanding and organisation of bodies in specific ways (Harding, J., 1993, 1997).

I am not concerned here with the 'accuracy' with which journalists report the findings of scientific research.[2] Rather, I am concerned with the published statements which are presumed to interest readers and how the production of these statements may incorporate and reproduce public concerns about and understandings of masculine embodiment. Newspapers inevitably make assumptions about their readers, their concerns and their 'reading positions' and, in doing so, help to create them. At the same time, texts are open to multiple readings by diverse and differently positioned readers, who are actively engaged in the production of meanings. That is to say, reception of messages is not a passive act of absorption. However, an analysis of what different readers make of specific texts is beyond the scope of this chapter.

The male body in theory/politics

In the last two decades, a huge amount of intellectual energy has gone into theorising 'the body' as a historical and political object and challenging its subordination to mind. Some theorists/activists have focused on the lived experience of embodiment, in particular that of marginalised groups (women, black people, lesbians and gays) where bodily experience is assumed to provide a foundation for a shared sense of identity and the articulation of common political goals and actions (often directed at a struggle for 'liberation'). Such emancipatory discourses do not usually speak of and to men's bodies. Arguably, modern western men have not had need of embodied political identities in the same way as, for example, the diversity of subjects categorised as 'women'.

In many discourses, modern men have been produced as *disembodied*. Indeed, this has been a crucial aspect of the Enlightenment values shaping modernity, in particular the idea that 'true' knowledge is 'objective' and produced through the correct use of reason. Reason is seen to exist independently of the self's contingent (bodily, historical, social) existence (Flax, 1990). In a series of crucial oppositional dualisms – mind/body, culture/nature, objectivity/subjectivity, reason/emotions, human/animal[3] – men have been aligned with mind/culture/reason/humanity and viewed as the only proper subjects of knowledge (Harding, S., 1986; Seidler, 1994). Men's sovereign capacity to reason has depended on the idea that they have the capacity to think and act independently of the historical and cultural contingencies of their bodies – to be effectively disembodied (Flax, 1990; Gallop, 1988; Seidler, 1994).

Such claims are not contradicted by numerous discourses – medical, aesthetic, political – on the male body which celebrate its strength, vigour, beauty, productivity, discipline and, sometimes, describe its deficiencies. Clearly, societies depend on the (re)productive forces and capacities of male as well as female bodies. Nations depend for their futures on *some* men having bodies with which to engage in battle and manual work. However, men's and cultures' relationship to these bodies appears to be one of distance and dominance as they are necessarily subjugated to thought. Rationality has been conceived as a relationship of superiority which has worked to legitimise a series of relationships of power whereby those considered closer to nature are subjugated and even, brutalised – for example, through colonialism and slavery (Seidler, 1994). Increasingly, some men (black, gay, poor, sick, imprisoned) draw attention to the specific (problematic) ways in which their bodies are signified. In doing so, they have indicated that masculine disembodiment in modernity is actually the idealised disembodiment of a few very privileged men (Western, middle class, white, heterosexual) who have depended on the embodiment of others (working class and black men and women) to labour so that they can be free to think (Gallop, 1988). The (dis)embodiment of men, then, is not consistent but culturally and historically variable.

The female body has been assumed to be a singular and constant entity that unites women and provides a foundation for feminist theory and politics. In contrast, Denise Riley argues that anyone's body is only periodically lived or treated as sexed (Riley, 1988: 103). It cannot be assumed that 'women's bodies are systematically and exhaustively differ- ent', or that they are 'unified in an integral otherness' (ibid.: 105). If, as Denise Riley writes, 'the sexed body is not something reliably constant' and is not capable of underpinning 'the thousand discourses on "women"' (ibid.: 106), is this also the case for subjects culturally positioned as 'men'? Probably not. To transpose this assertion to speak of men rather than women would be misleading because it is not certain that the categories male and female, men and women, are similarly 'subjected to a mono- lithic notion of sex' (Butler, 1992b: 346). More analysis is needed of the specific ways in which male bodies are invested.

Several arguments from contemporary feminist and lesbian and gay theory are useful to an analysis of the discursive production of bodies as male. Firstly, an uncritical use of identity categories tends to essentialise and consolidate (rather than deconstruct and change) the experience of those to whom they refer (Fuss, 1991; Scott, 1992). Secondly, a politics articulated through marginalised identity categories tends to reaffirm, rather than undermine, the centrality of that which it attempts to resist. That is, a focus on those marginalised by prevailing structures of domi- nance may leave 'the centre' undeconstructed and fail to shift prevailing power relations (Fuss, 1991). This thinking provides an imperative to scru- tinise what is taken to be at 'the centre' and to historicise the signifying practices through which specific identities are produced. Thirdly, identi- ties are not coherent and stable, but are multiple, fragmented and hybrid, fluctuating and intermittent (Riley, 1988; Rutherford, 1990a). Identities are invented through attempts to represent them and are always incomplete and always in process (Hall, 1990). This is the case in all representations, whether part of conservative or radical projects. Fourthly, identities must be 'performed' (Butler, 1990a). As I explained earlier, Judith Butler (1990a) argues that gender identity is not an attribute of an individual, but an act which much be repeatedly performed. Since gender performances are nei- ther arbitrary nor entirely elective, it is important to investigate the specific ways in which particular historical political discourses compel and constrain enactments of gendered identity and how some gendered meanings are contested and others affirmed. It is necessary to examine empirical examples. (These arguments are discussed in more detail in Chapter 4.)

The following discussion examines the ways in which discourses on environmental oestrogens 'sex' the male body and proceeds from the ideas that: (1) it is necessary to problematise, investigate and theorise masculine embodiment; (2) discourse has a productive and organising function; (3) the sexed body and the category 'men' can usefully be viewed as perfor- mance (as something that must be repeatedly produced through discourses which are both enabling and constraining); and (4) it is possible to view selected media texts as a series of (historically and culturally spe- cific) moments in the discursive production of understandings of the body, which compel both a limitation and an expansion of possible enactments whereby the body is configured as sexed.

Environmental oestrogens and 'feminisation'

you're only half the man you used to be . . . the sudden wave of publicity surrounding the announcement that the human sperm count has diminished by at least 50% in the last 50 years left us all feeling a little uncomfortable, men particularly . . . the guilty party could be oestrogen, the female sex hormone. (Lambton, 1993)

Oestrogen is commonly represented (in medical and other discourses) as the stereotypical 'female sex hormone' and the biological basis of femininity (Harding, J., 1996; Oudshoorn, 1994). Recently, it has been represented in media texts as an agent of disorder and sexual confusion. A focus on debate about the effects of environmental oestrogens on male bodies, and the discursive arrangement of bodies as male that this implies, also produces a particular configuration of the female body – usually as an encroaching and threatening environment. This debate has implications, therefore, for the constitution of all sexed subjects and, indeed, sexual difference.

The term 'environmental oestrogens' is widely deployed in media and scientific texts to refer to man-made and naturally occurring chemicals capable of disrupting 'the body's normal hormonal balance' by mimicking the actions of the female sex hormone oestrogen (Wright, 1996). The Institute for Environment and Health's report (1995) discussed the possible adverse effects of environmental oestrogens on the female reproductive and cardiovascular systems and breast cancer, but, together with media and pressure group commentaries, focuses more closely on possible consequences for the male body and men, in particular, the 'feminisation' of the male body.

The Institute for Environment and Health (IEH) report states that the available evidence supports 'a plausible hypothesis' that environmental oestrogens 'disrupt male reproductive function' (IEH, 1995: 2). The potential effects on males include reduced sperm counts and sperm quality, cryptorchidism (undescended testes), hypospadias (a congenital malformation of the penis), testicular cancer and male breast cancer (IEH, 1995). A statement by the environmental pressure group, Friends of the Earth, reported in the *Guardian*, identifies similar 'abnormalities' and also mentions 'small penises' and 'sterility' as possible consequences (*Guardian*, 25 July 1995). The IEH report is careful to state that there was no evidence as yet to support a *causal* link between so-called environmental oestrogens and the list of possible changes in male reproductive function (IEH, 1995: 2).[4] However, media and pressure group responses to the report appeared less circumspect, calling for *urgent* government action to protect the public from the 'gender-bending' effects of pollutants.

The IEH report suggests that external oestrogenic agents may effect the male both *in utero* by disturbing 'the hormonal secretions or actions necessary for male sexual differentiation' and *in adult life* by antagonising the release or activity of testosterone, leading to 'feminisation and reduced spermatogenesis' (IEH, 1995: 13). Oestrogens are reported to enter the adult male body from the external environment via synthetic oestrogens, oestrogens occurring naturally in edible plant stuffs and chemical compounds (with oestrogenic properties).[5] It was suspected (but not proven) that constituents and breakdown products of the contraceptive pill may enter the environment through sewage effluent and drinking water. In addition, oestrogens in the environment are reported to result from 'significant concentrations of oestradiol and oestrone' naturally excreted by pregnant women and female animals (IEH, 1995: 26).

Other (scientific) texts support the claim that the male is exposed *in utero* to an excess of oestrogen by the maternal body. Women (like men) are said to be exposed to environmental oestrogens via diet, drinking water and environmental contamination and, in addition, to be exposed to (their own) *endogenous oestrogens*, which are metabolised less well on a modern Western high fat, low fibre, diet (Sharpe and Skakkebaek, 1993). It has been suggested that it is not unlikely that 'the increasing incidence of reproductive abnormalities in the human male' is related to 'increased oestrogen exposure in utero' during foetal development over the last 40–50 years, since 'humans now live in an environment that can be viewed as a virtual sea of oestrogens' (Sharpe and Skakkebaek, 1993: 1392).

In the last three and a half years, press coverage of the possible effects of 'environmental oestrogens' (including, most recently, 'phthalates' in infant formula)[6] has been organised around a limited range of concepts, propositions and attention-grabbing phrases which crop up again and again. The terms 'gender-bending chemicals', 'infertility', 'feminisation' and 'demasculinisation' are frequently used to refer to the dangers posed to the male body and masculinity by environmental oestrogens. How do these terms function to facilitate specific configurations of the sexed body and gender? That is, sex/ualities? How do these configurations compel and constrain gender performances?

All newspaper texts examined here focus on reports of falling sperm counts amongst different populations of human males, and malformations and malfunctions of male reproductive organs. They also cite laboratory experiments linking compounds capable of mimicking oestrogen – 'the female sex hormone' – with reduction of sperm counts and testicle size in laboratory rats. Such observations are interpreted and highlighted as evidence of a progressive 'feminisation' and 'demasculinisation' of human males.

Gruner and Revill wrote an article entitled 'Infertility due to "gender-bender drugs"', describing 'the hazard posed by "gender-bending" chemicals that can alter sexual characteristics' (Gruner and Revill, 1995). A pollution campaigner for Friends of the Earth is quoted by Gruner and Revill as saying: 'The effects we are talking about are the growing of breasts, and the development of female sexual organs as well as the suppression of the growth of male sexual organs'. Anne Johnstone, writing in the *Herald*, quotes a Greenpeace advertisement which boldly states 'You're not half the man your father was' and informed readers that 'there has been a decline in sperm quality as well as quantity. Many simply aren't up to the job. They don't swim strongly enough or haven't the strength to penetrate the ovum' (Johnstone, 1995).[7]

Interestingly, in the above text, sperm are invested with a mission which is already gendered. Sperm are expected to 'behave' in ways deemed culturally characteristic of men and masculine heterosexuality. That is, they are expected to display strength and vigour and to replicate the (procreative) heterosexual act from (and constituting) a masculine point of view, typified by penetration. In this way, masculinity is inscribed on minute biological objects and processes which operate both as bearers of the cultural meanings of masculinity and, importantly, constitute their origins in nature (because biology is accepted as *the* discourse on life in its pre-cultural, natural state). Sperm thereby become inscribed as natural objects and originators of the social organisation of gender.

In summer 1996, according to John Emsley writing in the *Independent*, 'Britain was gripped by the fear that substances called phthalates could be contaminating infant formula feeds'. The new 'scare' was prompted by the fear that these were 'gender-bending' chemicals. 'Phthalates', again, are described as chemicals which mimic the 'female hormone' oestrogen and are seen as being particularly harmful for male babies. It was suggested that they might 'impair fertility' (Press Association, 1996), 'cause cancer and infertility' (Sears and Little, 1996), be linked to 'impaired infertility' (Cooper, 1996), cause 'cancer and bizarre sex changes in birds and fish' (Morris, 1996), and bring about 'feminising effects, potentially leading to reduced fertility in males' (Lawson, 1996).

Journalists report that, when levels of phthalates similar to those found in samples of infant formula were administered to baby rats in tests by the Medical Research Council (MRC), 'their testicles were damaged and sperm counts reduced' (Delgardo and Clarke, 1996; Jenkins and Nuttall, 1996; Marks and Copley, 1996). Jenkins and Nuttall writing in *The Times* (1996) state that 'phthalates' have been linked by 'researchers around the world' to 'an increase in cases of undescended testes, a lowering of sperm counts and a rise in female breast cancer'.

The chemicals have been discovered in every sample of different baby milks tested. And the levels of them are worryingly close to those that have caused testicles to shrink and sperm counts to drop in laboratory rats. This is the most alarming evidence to date that whole families of chemicals, spread through the environment, may be threatening our very future. (Lean, 1996)

The texts considered here repeatedly articulated concern that environmental oestrogens might be 'disrupting' a (natural) hormonal balance in males and compromising their very 'maleness', through the additive effects of an excess of oestrogen and its capacity to 'inhibit' and 'antagonise' the actions of male hormones. Reduced sperm 'quantity' and 'quality' and 'damaged' or 'shrunken' testicles signify the sexed body in danger. Reproduction is made a defining characteristic of masculinity and male (hetero)sexuality, which in turn is discursively 'produced' as absolutely necessary to the future of *humanity*. This discourse references the biological body as the exclusive site at which gender is being 'bent'. It is worth considering whether this biological body may be a conduit for discussing contemporary (re)organisations of gender in a variety of arenas (for example, at home and at work). Are women perceived as 'too much' and 'too powerful' and, consequently, as inhibiting and downgrading men?

'Intersexed', 'hermaphrodite' and 'lesbian' wildlife – evidence of gender-bending

Journalists consistently assumed that, under certain circumstances, laboratory animals, and wildlife, may both reflect the past and predict the future for humans. Texts appear to speak to readers' worst fears about the possible effects of 'gender-bending chemicals' by citing evidence of 'sex changes' in wild animals and implying that these reveal what lies ahead for human males. Statements about sex changes in wildlife form the basis for the emphatic claim that environmental oestrogens are, in fact, 'gender-benders'. In relating observed changes in the sexual organs, fertility and mating patterns in wildlife, texts elaborate the possible meanings of the term 'gender-bending'.

> It sounds the stuff of science fiction, yet it is the soberest of fact: male fish turn female, alligators' penises shrivel, sperm dies and cancer grows, a strange plague visited upon modern society . . . . (*Scotsman*, 1995)

Lawrence Wright, writing in the *Guardian* in March 1996, cites the findings of John Sumpter, a fish biologist from Brunel University, that 'a number of fish in British rivers and streams have turned up with odd-looking genitalia – they were suffering from a condition called intersex – that is, they contained the genitals of both sexes'. Wright goes on to report that 'below sewage outfall in northern England', investigators have found that 'one in 20 fish were hermaphrodites'. Along with other journalists he reports further observations.

> There are isolated examples of other animals in nature that are experiencing reproductive problems quite similar to man's, including decreased fertility and

sex reversals. As a result of the dumping over more than two decades of DDT into the Los Angeles sewer system, female western gulls – they have come to be known as lesbian gulls – took to nesting together, because the males had apparently lost interest. (Wright, 1996)

The effects of spillage (of dicofil containing DDT) from a chemical mixing plant into Lake Apopka in Florida was to deplete the alligator population:

Researchers have found that oestrogen levels in female hatching alligators are nearly twice what they should have been, and the ovaries of juveniles appear burned out – as if menopausal. The males register practically no testosterone. Penis sizes are smaller . . . three quarters to two-thirds of what they used to be. (ibid.)

This discussion relies upon a model of hormonally determined sex, in which the sex hormones, oestrogen and testosterone, appear antagonistic and the property of *one* sex. The implication is that these hormones 'function separately and exclusively to "sex" subjects' (Harding, J., 1996: 100), despite a contrary biomedical discourse which states that oestrogens are present and functional in both male and female bodies (Harding, J., 1996; Vines, 1993). Journalists' discussion of sex changes in wildlife relies upon and reinforces the notion that hormones determine sex and that sex can be readily diagnosed via a visual inspection of the individual body and its genitals. The size, form and function of the organs supposed to signify sex are highlighted and inscribed as the bodily, biological and universal foundation of normal masculinity and femininity, which are finally confirmed through heterosexual coupling. Disruptions of the sequence of events, linking sex organs to gender and sexuality, and possible ambiguities are seen as self-evident causes for alarm. Sex hormones are positioned both as the origins of sex and agents which confer (pre-existing) notions of what sex *is* (Harding, J., 1996). However, the idea of sex and the sequence of events it is said to cause only makes sense in terms of the prior establishment of the regime of heterosexuality which it is said to cause (Butler, 1990a; Foucault, 1981).

Animals have been used in experiments as evidence for sexual difference and heterosexual normality as if this were autonomously articulated by experimental animals and wildlife – rather than being shaped, as some argue, by the projections of experimenters and observers. These projections involve imposing on individual animals highly specific assumptions about the dichotomous nature of sex, and what constitutes normal femininity and masculinity, within human economies of heterosexuality (Birke and Vines, 1987: 560). This is illustrated in the above excerpts from Wright's article in the *Guardian*, which interprets, represents and constructs the behaviour of 'female western gulls' in the crude stereotypical terms in which lesbianism is commonly signified: as a last resort, a second-rate sexuality based on failure to attract interested males.

'Wildlife' functions as a litmus test of the extent to which nature has been distorted and corrupted by humans and demonstrates what the future holds for human males. As Donna Haraway points out, animals have continued to have a special status as 'natural objects that can show people their origin and therefore their pre-rational, pre-management, pre-cultural essence' (Haraway, 1991: 11). In discourses on the effects of environmental oestrogens, animals also appear to predict a post-management chaotic state of being.

Ambiguous natural environments

Media texts articulate a persistent sense of horror at ambiguity 'in nature'. Nature connotes both a threat to and nurturing of health and life. In the context of discourse on environmental oestrogens, nature is both a rural and a maternal environment. Both connote a place of refuge and a source of danger which threatens the (masculine) subject's identity.

The term 'nature' has been used in modernity to mean the countryside – 'the unspoiled places, plants and creatures other than man' (Williams, 1976: 186). In some discourses of modernity, it has been romantically posed in contrast to overcrowded, polluted and dangerous cities. Now, it seems, the countryside is not safe. Many man-made hazards emanate from the rural environment as a result of the disposal of industrial waste, pollution of rivers and soil and the effects of this on wildlife and agricultural practices.

The maternal body is especially dangerous since if 'even a small amount of an extraneous synthetic oestrogen slips across the mother's placental boundary at a critical moment and invades the body of a developing foetus, it can have a devastating impact on male sexual development . . . of all the hormones we know, the oestrogens are the most potent' (Wright, 1996).

> It is disturbing to realise that these oestrogen-like chemicals can pass undetected through a mother's body, creating havoc in the developing foetus. (ibid.)

The imagery used is militaristic. Oestrogens are the enemy bound to attack. The mother must protect the unborn male, but is a corrupt border guard who allows the enemy to slip across and cause havoc as sexual difference is (allegedly) disrupted. Perhaps what disturbs most is a sense of duplicity: the otherwise protective and life sustaining environment, the mother's body, threatens males when they are at their most vulnerable and dependent and undermines their essential maleness. The placental boundary, which marks out a safe place for the foetus and separates it as an entity from the mother's body, is breached. Literally surrounded (and overwhelmed) by the maternal body, the male (foetal) subject is represented as betrayed and powerless.

Fears about 'gender bending', in both maternal and external environments, resonate with fears about loss of identity which Julia Kristeva characterises in the concept *abjection*. According to Kristeva, the maternal body symbolises the threat of the other to the subject and encroaches on the subject's identity as a sea of non-identity (Kristeva, 1982; Grosz, 1990).[8] 'A sea of oestrogen' appears to threaten the masculine subject with engulfment in non-identity and non-difference. It signifies the inherent dangers of the maternal body stemming from an excess of oestrogens both contained within and excreted beyond its boundaries. In weighing up the threats to masculinity, the texts construct a singular coherent version of the male body, distinguished from an opposing signified body. The male body is at sea and, engulfed by a maternal body, potentially fails to develop differently.

All aspects of mothering, variously connected with the maternal body, are implicated. The gestating mother exposes her male foetus to endogenous and exogenous (environmental) oestrogens which are the sum effects of living a contemporary biologically female body. The breastfeeding mother continues to expose him to the hazards she harbours in her body. The mother who bottle-feeds (and it is assumed to be mainly a mother's responsibility) adds a further hazard – phthalates, which contaminate infant formula. The food (and the mother who gives it) intended to nurture and sustain life, it seems, might actually compromise it.

> The emotive impact is potentially enormous: a central image of humankind (and, of course, of infant formula advertising), that of a little baby sucking life-giving milk, suddenly contaminated. There is a special irony in this latest health alert: the very substance which sustains this generation of babies may, it is now alleged, be preventing the procreation of the next. (*Scotsman*, 1996)

> Parents have few fears worse than of unwittingly feeding their babies with something that will stop them growing into true men or women. Their nightmare approached reality this weekend with the revelation that Government scientists have found alarming levels of 'gender-bending' chemicals in baby milk. (Lean, 1996)

Clearly, concerns about infant formula are also part of an ongoing debate about the relative advantages and disadvantages of breast- versus bottle-feeding. However, the point is that maternal nurturing, by whatever means, is seen to pose risks to masculine sexual identity. Mothers are thereby rendered responsible for the production and maintenance of sexual difference – of producing the next generation of 'true' men and women. (Interestingly, no journalist explored the implications of 'gender-bending' chemicals for 'women to be'.)

Reproductive (hetero) sex/uality and powerlessness

All texts appear to address worried male readers (and their potentially guilty mothers and partners) and position them as struggling for survival *as* men. At risk, together with the future of men, is the future of humanity/ the species: 'men will become infertile by the middle of the next century unless certain man-made chemicals are banned', since they are 'threatening the fertility, intelligence and survival of the human species' (Allen, 1996a).

Texts emphasise the essential role of men in reproduction and of reproduction to the essential nature of men. Men are also constituted as responsible for the continuation of the human species and, somewhat arrogantly, for its *intelligence*. However, men are also positioned as relatively *powerless* in the face of a danger which is said to be coming from everywhere. Journalists articulate concern about the sheer size of the problem under discussion – the number of man-made chemicals in use and the extent to which they are spread through the environment – and an underlying fear that it may not be possible to detect them and undo their adverse effects. Most journalists stress the ubiquitous nature of hormone-disrupting chemicals, their excessive presence in our bodies due to their widespread use in industry and domestic products and their presence in foodstuffs and drinking water.

Journalists inform readers that: up to 500 hormone-disrupting chemicals may be present in our bodies (Allen, 1996a); 3,000 different chemicals are utilised in industry and domestic products (*Scotsman*, 1995); and a possible list of 100,000 chemicals on the market may have a medical effect (Connor, 1995). Robert Allen (1996b) writes that in 1990 there were 'more than 600 million alkyphenol polyethoxylates in use globally' (alkyphenols have been implicated as environmental oestrogens).

Possible sources of hormone-disrupting chemicals include: pregnant women; fatty diets; by-products of petrol and plastics industries, contraceptive pills excreted into water supplies imbibed by men, cow's milk (the dairy industry has produced cows that lactate when pregnant which produces milk rich in oestrogens, beans and pulses: Lambton, 1993).

> It is as if manhood itself were waging a losing campaign against forces as yet unknown but frighteningly overwhelming. (Wright, 1996)

Whilst another voice is clearly audible within these texts, saying that a reduction in fertility on a global scale might not be such a bad thing and might even be desirable, there is an awkward articulation between the individual and the global entity, private and public concerns. A sense of gendered alarm persists.

To offset these concerns, some writers offer a detailed account of the sheer magnitude of the male contribution to the process of reproduction. They stress the enormous volume of sperm produced and their strength and determination in achieving conception. Whilst it is acknowledged that the majority of sperm are redundant (one, rather than the millions that are produced, is needed if and when conception is desired, which it is mostly not), the quantity and quality of sperm are emphatically linked, in fantasy if not in fact, with fertility and virility and come to signify masculinity.

In contrast to this emphasis on the significance of individual male con-tributions, contemporary debates about new reproductive technologies (NRTs), much discussed in the press, express concerns about an apparent reduction in male input into (postmodern) reproduction. The use of various NRTs to assist conception fracture an imagined continuum self-evidently linking male and female bodies with the expression of (hetero)sexuality, eventually confirmed by the birth of a baby.

Although use of NRTs is not widespread, awareness of them is.[9] New reproductive technologies enable reproduction to occur apart from any heterosexual act, without personal possession of the requisite body parts (sperm and ova) which may be donated from a known or unknown source, and without male partners, in the case of lesbian couples and single (lesbian or straight) women (this is discussed further in Chapter 8). In some well publicised quarters, it would appear that men – or, at least, the specificities of male body parts and heterosexual desire – are becoming less central to the reproduction of the species.

Out with a wimp?

Generally, newspaper texts vary according to the level of scientific detail reproduced and the extent to which it is critiqued.[10] They vary in their stance on environmental politics and lifestyles – is this just a fact (to be accepted) of late twentieth-century urban industrial living or a matter for global environmental action? Texts also vary in the precise assumptions they make about the meanings of falling sperm counts and whether or not this adds up to 'male infertility'. However, different assumptions about readers' prior knowledge, desire for scientific detail and political concerns are overidden by common themes and messages.

These texts are saturated by a discourse which is overwhelmingly con-cerned with reductions in size of male sex organs and falling sperm counts and quality. This flood of discourse is extremely repetitive and says little that is new. Most texts compare worldwide statistics to show that sperm counts have declined by 50 per cent in the past 50 years. Whilst some journalists indicate that scientific evidence does not show that falling sperm counts and quality spell infertility for all men, most journalists do dwell at length on what they consider to be the alarming prospect of male infertility. They imply that infertility is (about to become) generic. They all reiterate the assumption that infertility is fem-inising/ demasculinising for men by virtue of an assumed (causal) link between masculine identity, male (hetero)sexuality and procreation. Fertility appears to be affirmative and constitutive of masculine identity (men as men) and masculine sexuality (assumed to be heterosexual). Hence, the repeated reference to being 'half the man' (you or your father *were*) or being especially 'macho' or being 'true men' or 'wimps' on the basis of sperm counts.

New York men probably felt more macho than usual last week after hearing they have higher sperm counts than males in other US cities. (Dillner, 1996)

Evidence is growing that they [phthalates] may be behind a precipitous plunge in fertility – the average man now produces only a third as much sperm as a hamster – rising cancers, and weird sex changes in wildlife. They raise the chance, as T. S. Eliot might have said, that the world will indeed end not with a bang, but with a wimp. (Lean, 1996)

In the above statements, the cultural values of what it means to be a man are inscribed on specific body parts (such as size of sex organs and quantity of sperm) and minute biological processes which are credited with causing major social consequences, such as the social organisation of gender. The suggestion that the world might end 'not with a bang, but with a wimp' constitutes a discursive manoeuvre which again renders masculine (procreative) heterosexual desire responsible for the future of humanity and characterises it as forceful, powerful, even violent (hence, 'bang'). 'Wimp' connotes the collapse of sexual difference as a result of the demasculinisation/ feminisation of men thanks to oestrogen which, in this context, stands for all that is feminine and, consequently, encroaching and colonising. Concerns about sterility operate to reassert a logic in which sex is already written on the body, and subsequently expressed as a gender, then as a sexual desire which finds its ultimate expression in reproduction (Butler, 1990a). Procreation confirms the expression of desire as heterosexual and reaffirms the binary categories of sex which necessarily support it (Butler, 1990a; Foucault, 1981).

Sexing the body

How are enactments of sex/uality compelled and constrained in these texts? How is the male body configured?

The demasculinisation and feminisation of the male body is claimed to consist of falling sperm counts and smaller/damaged sexual organs. Evidence cited from other species (who are variously described as intersexed, hermaphrodite, lesbian) justifies the use of the terms 'gender-bending' chemicals and 'sex-change' chemicals. The male body is produced as relatively powerless in the face of dangerous environments – post-industrial urban and rural landscapes and the maternal body – and at work and play in the processes of production, reproduction and consumption. Its very maleness is being compromised by ubiquitous invisible, often undetected, chemical agents.

Biological categories and processes are made central to configurations of the sexed body. This body is represented as properly either male or female as a result of action by hormones which are already themselves always either male or female (Harding, J., 1996). The female body is configured as an encroaching, colonising space. Oestrogen connotes the essence of femininity, which is not adequately contained within the boundaries of the female body but transmitted to the male body directly in pregnancy and via the external environment, threatening to produce a world that is devoid of sexual difference – feminised or genderless.

By deploying the terms 'gender-bending' chemicals and 'sex-change' chemicals, the texts appear to evoke and speak to their audiences' worst fears: the feminisation of the global environment and collapse of sexual difference. Concerns about gender bending in the statements of journalists centre on the perceived potential of oestrogens to erode bodily borders supporting sexual difference and, explicitly, masculine sex/uality. These observations appear to be constituted from and to constitute a specifically and singularly masculine subject position. The effects of this reporting are to restate the terms of sexual difference as necessarily discrete, opposing and hormonally determined. Whilst the texts construct the heterosexual reproductive body as the ultimate expression of sexual difference, there is a palpable tension – this body does not exist permanently and for certain, it has to be repeatedly reinvented and enacted.

The end of the world?

The sheer volume of discourse on the effects of environmental oestrogens on male bodies and the endless repetition of the same terms and propositions suggest that journalists are speaking to the perceived fears of readers about a world of genderlessness, where masculine identity and sexuality is erased by the feminine. The faint presence of other discourses (on the problems of worldwide overpopulation, whether the threat to fertility is 'real', voluntary childlessness) does not detract from the overriding impression produced of the colonising potential of the female body. Why do journalists want to write about this?

Discussion about the possible feminisation and demasculinisation of men may well reflect concerns about genderlessness thought to result from the perceived collapse of gendered hierarchies in some public and domestic contexts.[11] This is not to say that gender inequalities have disappeared but that changing patterns of employment may have affected men in ways they have not previously experienced (unemployment, temporary, part-time and piece work). Interestingly, journalists identify and name specific sources of environmental oestrogens, whilst, at the same time, insisting that they are generalised, decentred and come from everywhere. In this way, they actively construct a chaotic situation and a position of powerlessness for men.

Perceptions of social chaos – brought about through changes in gender roles and possible moves towards 'genderlessness' – may be more easily expressed in terms of biological processes. Biological discourse is the twentieth-century discourse for speaking about and organising the body. It is used to invest the body with sexed meanings. Biological processes may act as both a metaphor for what is thought to be happening and as a means of reinvesting/reinscribing cultural values and ideas regarding sexual difference. That is to say, 'the biological' may operate as a container for cultural and emotional concerns, making them seem more tangible, more objective and, consequently, available to scientific intervention and mediation. Biological discourse may articulate the precariousness of sex/uality and offer some hope of redemption by appealing to modernist beliefs in science as a means to progressive mastery over nature and adversity (already highly gendered).

I have analysed specific texts (discussing 'environmental oestrogens') for the various ways in which they produce the sexed body, thereby compelling and constraining further bodily performances. The texts show how a public articulation of concern about the maintenance of sexual difference may be part of its repeated enactment. My readings of these media texts are necessarily incomplete and do not, for example, investigate how readers read these messages and use them in reinventing gender identities.

In the next chapter I examine the production of reproductive sex/uality in discourses which address 'women' as mothers.

Notes

1. This analysis is based on a total of 54 articles found in a search of UK newspapers between January 1993 and September 1996.

2. I am not suggesting that this is unimportant, simply that it is not my concern here.

3. These oppositional dualisms operate as key organising principles in the structures of modernity and its scientific and philosophical traditions.

4. The report concludes that, although animal studies support a plausible hypothesis that oestrogens, or possible anti-androgens, disrupt male reproductive function, 'there is as yet no evidence that the effects recognised in the human population are necessarily causally linked to the presence of such chemicals in the environment' (IEH, 1995: 2). More research is called for to explore possible causal links. It is not clear whether there is a common cause of male reproductive abnormalities, since many factors could have 'effected changes in hormonal status of populations in recent times, including changes in life style, dietary intakes and use of oral contraceptives' (IEH, 1995: 23).

5. They 'may mimic or interfere with the action of endogenous oestrogenic hormones' and their effects may be additive, synergistic or inhibitory (IEH, 1995: 24–5).

6. It has been claimed that 'phthalates' in infant formula 'may have weak oestrogenic activity' (Jenkins and Nuttall, 1996).

7. 'Responsibility' for infertility appears to have become shared *more* equally between men and women. According to Johnstone, 'in our parents' generation the male side of the equation was reckoned to account for just 10% of infertility in couples. Now it's 25% and growing' (Johnstone, 1995).

8. The maternal space is a constantly collapsing relation between subject and object, self and body, in which separateness disappears (Kristeva, 1982: 64–72).

9. Access to NRTs is usually restricted to those who can afford to pay for them. Individual clinics and clinicians may specify which groups 'qualify' for treatment. Some specify that women should be below a certain age, be married or in a stable heterosexual relationship.

10. Broadsheet and tabloid newspapers vary in the detail in which they discuss scientific studies and the validity and reliability of their often contradictory findings comparing sperm counts across time and culture. Some highlight problems with research on the basis of differences and disparities in measuring techniques used.

11. Many other avenues could be explored here. For example, a focus on changes in biological processes as a result of environmental oestrogens may also contain an implicit social message about public health and government failure to protect populations.

7

SEX/UALITY AND THE MATERNAL BODY

Mother figures

The figure of 'mother' is a very powerful and significant player in the construction and regulation of contemporary sex/ualities. Mother is understood as equivalent to woman (and the feminine) and to exhaust its possible meanings. The maternal body can be understood as 'an effect or consequence of a system of sexuality in which the female body is required to assume maternity as the essence of itself and the law of its desire' (Butler, 1990a: 92). The maternal body is a crucial support for a regime of heterosexuality and the binary categorisation of sex. It signifies and consolidates a causal relation between sex, gender and sexuality.

In *The History of Sexuality*, Foucault discusses 'four strategic unities which, beginning in the eighteenth century, formed specific mechanisms of knowledge and power centering on sex' (Foucault, 1981: 103). Two of these strategies bear directly on reproductive sexuality and, in particular, on the reproductive female body: the 'hysterization of women's bodies' and the 'socialisation of procreative behaviour'. These processes rendered women's bodies available to multi-pronged interventions to control and regulate them as part of a deployment of sexuality designed to maintain the 'homeostasis of the social body'. 'The mother' represented the most visible form of 'hysterization'. The maternal body was also 'targeted' through the 'socialisation of procreative behaviour' whereby couples came under economic, social, political and medical pressure to exercise responsibility towards the social body as a whole and to limit or reinvigorate their fertility accordingly (Foucault, 1981: 104–7).

The figure of the mother, and other figures mentioned by Foucault (the masturbating child, the Malthusian couple, the perverse adult), are produced through historically specific discursive formations focused (obsessively) on sex. As I said earlier, discourses systematically form and order, within relations of power, the objects of which they speak (Foucault, 1986). Indeed, 'discourses create what it is possible to think by articulating different elements into a discursive formation at particular times'

(Woodward, 1997: 255). Kathryn Woodward suggests that the figure of the mother can be thought of as a recurring subject position 'produced through different discourses and at multiple institutional points – by parents, families, doctors, psychologists' (ibid.).

Medical and scientific discourses, which claim to discover objective knowledge about sexuality, have been the most influential and authoritative in the construction of the figure of mother. These discourses have, as Foucault suggests, pathologised the maternal body and defined it as needing treatment and regulation. Biomedical discourses have also helped to 'naturalise' the maternal body, rendering it an inevitable, ahistorical, essential characteristic of 'woman', by virtue of their authority to describe and explain the truth about 'life'. It is a medicalised version of motherhood which tends to be promulgated at different institutional sites. This version of motherhood tends to be represented as a single and coherent identity. Also, motherhood and mothers tend to be the objects of discourse – being spoken about and to by experts: 'mother' rarely refers to positions from which individuals make authoritative statements.

If mothers exist at the juncture of various discourses which address and position them as such, it is important to ask to what extent and how do individuals recognise themselves in these figures/positions? Can they speak as mothers? To what extent has sexual politics opened up new (maternal) speaking positions?

The strategic unities described by Foucault, and the recurring subject position mentioned by Woodward, can be seen as attempts at re-enactments (performances) which are never quite the same, although embodying many similarities. The figure of mother, as a discursive and historical product, can be seen to be an unstable, multiple and contested identity. Different discourses produce different versions of the mother and sexualised subject positions. In the rest of this chapter, I examine selected discourses on maternity and the sex/ualities they imply.

The medicalisation of the maternal body

How is the figure of mother, 'thoroughly saturated with sexuality', produced through contemporary medical discourse and the discourses of sexual and reproductive politics? How does 'bio-politics' work through medical discourse on the sexuality of women and resistances to this?

The concept of 'medicalisation' is a useful starting point. 'Medicalisation' has been a central theme in sociological and feminist writings about medicine and the medical profession since the 1970s (Harding, J., 1993; Lupton, 1995b; 1997). The 'medicalisation critique' identified a paradox: 'medicine as it is practiced in Western societies, despite its alleged lack of effectiveness in treating a wide range of conditions and its iatrogenic side-effects, has increasingly amassed power and influence' (Lupton, 1997: 95). Social life and social problems have increasingly become 'viewed through the prism of medicine as "diseases"' (ibid.), that is, 'medicalised'. 'Medicalisation' is seen to *disempower* and to undermine the autonomy of the individual in dealing with his or her own problems. Members of the medical profession are seen as enhancing their own already powerful positions by assuming the exclusive right to diagnose and treat illness (ibid.: 96). Patients from disadvantaged groups, from the perspective of the medicalisation critique, are vulnerable in interactions with doctors when they seek medical attention because they lack medical knowledge.

The 'medicalisation critique' is not new. Twenty years ago, Irving Zola argued that medicine was becoming a 'major institution of social control', nudging aside religion and the law, and the 'new repository of truth, the place where absolute and final judgements are made by supposedly morally neutral and objective experts'. These judgements are made 'in the name of health'. This phenomenon has occurred not through the political power of doctors but is 'largely an insidious and often undramatic phenomenon accomplished by "medicalizing" much of daily living, by making medicine and the labels "healthy" and "ill" *relevant* to an ever increasing part of human existence' (Zola, 1978: 80). The labels 'health' and 'illness' depoliticise issues by locating them in individuals, so closing off other levels of intervention, effectively deflecting inquiry from various social inequalities. Zola argued that 'by the very acceptance of a specific behavior as an "illness", and the definition of illness as an undesirable state, the issue becomes not whether to deal with a particular problem, but *how* and *when*' (ibid.: 95). The medicalising of society is about medicine's potential and a social desire to use that potential.

Homosexuality, contraception and abortion, pregnancy and childbirth, for example, once defined as problematic aspects of sexuality and as illness, are then rendered available to medical intervention.

Feminists writing about women's sexuality and reproductive politics have argued that women in particular have been subject to medicalisation. It is argued that women's lives are almost entirely medicalised because 'normal' and 'natural' physiological processes like menstruation, pregnancy, childbirth and menopause are defined as pathological and in need of treatment (Coney, 1991; Klein, 1992; Martin, 1989; Worcester and Whately, 1992; Zita, 1988). Medicalisation, it is argued, disempowers women and contributes to their continuing subjugation.

Detailed examples of how women's bodies and sexualities are brought under medical surveillance, pathologised and regulated – how bio-politics might actually work – are the result of particular forms of feminist struggle over the last few decades aimed at gaining reproductive and sexual rights and freedoms.

Jacqueline Zita conceptualises *medicalisation* (in her analysis of the emergence of premenstrual syndrome: PMS) as a process whereby 'subjectively expressed meanings voiced by women' are codified into 'quantifiable symptoms and signs' sharing a common pattern of premenstrual cyclicity.

The medicalised female body, constituted as an object of interest for the medical gaze, is removed from the social and ideological contexts in which it is lived and interpreted. It is problematised as 'an aggregate of clinically detectable organic or psychogenic events' for which causes are located within its boundaries. Thus, clinical discourse provides objective and scientific legitimation for sexist interpretations of women's bodies and actions in everyday discourse, where negative evaluations and 'complaints' requiring medical redefinition are formulated (Zita, 1988: 85–90).

In *The Woman in the Body* (1989), Emily Martin examines the scientific representation of women's bodies, analysing metaphors and imagery used in medical textbooks to describe menstruation, childbirth and menopause. She argues that negative imagery is used to describe specifically female bodily processes (to do with reproduction) which are represented as needing to be managed and corrected. Martin suggests, 'dominant medical metaphors' produce women's bodies in menstruation, birth and menopause as 'a hierarchical system of centralised control organised for the purpose of efficient production and speed' and produce 'breakdown, decay, failure or inefficiency' as grounds for medical attention (Martin, 1989: 66). In medical textbooks, menstrual blood is constructed as a catastrophic disintegration, producing haemorrhage and necrosis (death of tissue), and represents the wasted, failed or wrongful production of a system designed to make a baby.[1]

According to Martin, modern science and medicine have contributed to the fragmentation of the unity of the person by treating the body as a machine to be fixed by the physician-as-technician. In relation to birth, the uterus is seen as an involuntary muscle which the doctor manages through mechanical and pharmacological manipulations while the woman labours. The baby is the *product* (Martin, 1989: 64). Medical texts focus on tools for extracting the foetus and prescriptions for time and motion progression of labour and birth. Doctors are concerned with foetal outcome. Caesarian section involves the most management by doctors and least labour by women and is seen as producing the best results – based on the notion that normal labour is unnecessarily traumatic to the baby. This takes the focus away from the mother and delivery towards foetal outcome. A space is opened for the doctor to ally with the baby against the potential destruction wreaked upon it by the mother's body. Mother/baby are seen as a conflicting dyad rather than an integral unit.

> The organic unity of fetus and mother can no longer be assumed, and all these newly fragmented parts can now be subjected to market forces, ordered, produced, bought and sold. (Martin, 1989: 20)

As in other forms of industrialised labour, women experience alienation from 'the product' of labour because of their lack of involvement and because their work is controlled and regimented.

So what versions of mother (the body thoroughly saturated with sexuality) are produced by the medicalisation critique? How are 'women'
variously positioned?

Reproductive sexuality has been a major focus of critiques of medicine
and sexual politics, as feminists have deconstructed ideologies of motherhood (impelling women to be mothers, designating what that should entail
in terms of the limited roles of good or bad mother and what that involves),
revealing motherhood to be an institution of social control over women,
and, alternatively, celebrating motherhood as an essential characteristic of
women and a basis of women's identity (Woodward, 1997: 241).

(Some) feminist, sociological, anthropological writings reproduce essentialised versions of 'woman' and/or 'woman' as a passive subject
position – the non-speaking objects of an oppressing discourse. The
female body represents a basic sameness shared by women and the foundation for the variations and coincidences of experience which is capable
of uniting them socially and politically. Thus, Martin suggests that
women's bodily processes can be reinscribed and valorised rather than
denigrated. For example, menstrual blood can be seen as 'making the life
stuff that marks us as women or heralding our non-pregnant state'.
Menstruation could be described as 'an emblem of women's particular
experience of the world' and a basis for common action. It designates 'the
true unity women have: we menstruate or have menstruated in the
past . . . [it is] the one thing we all share, fertile, infertile, heterosexual,
homosexual' (Martin, 1989: 111–12).

In this way, Martin constructs an essentially sexed reproductive body in
common for women by stating that 'all have female bodies and experience
common bodily processes' such as menstruation, childbirth and menopause
(Martin, 1989: 4–5). A pre-existing body already arranged as sexed and
reproductive is brought into being as the object of the opposing characterisations: negative medical imagery versus positive alternative visions. The
body thus constituted is a collection of processes and givens variously available to differing interpretations and representations. Reinscriptions (like
emphasising the excess and magnitude of ova) as a solution to a common
problem, further constitute all women as similarly denigrated by virtue of,
and constituting, a pre-existing reproductive body in common. The deployment of 'experience' in this context functions to essentialise women because
bodily sameness is assumed to be the ground for a wealth of experience.

The 'medicalisation critique' produces a medicalised body and, conversely, an unmedicalised/natural body. It also promotes oppositions
between clinical and everyday discourse, men and women. This strategy
constitutes women patients or potential patients as a homogeneous group,
with common interests and relations to clinical encounters, symptom nar-
ratives, men and idealised unmedicalised lives. It constructs a singular
female body based on common experience of 'normal physiological
processes'. It does not easily take account of how relations of power shape
the different subject positions from which women may seek to negotiate or

reject clinical verdicts and procedures, nor the subject positions excluded by a focus on the clinic and resistance to medical control. In many circumstances, though aware of its limits, women seek medical treatment as the only or preferred option.

In many women's health texts, disease and sex are constructed as exclusive of each other and reproduction is seen as their major meeting point. In these texts, disease is produced as a site of negativity, reprisal and repression, where power flows only in one direction, exerted by medical expert over the generic woman patient. Medical observation and explanation are constituted as imposed on passive and unwilling bodies. Disease is a result of sexism which is secondary to and presupposes the coherence and fixity of an underlying sexed body. Further, a persistent challenge by women's health discourse to the diseasing of (normal) reproductive bodily processes, and insistence that these are not really diseases, implies that somewhere else there exist other 'real' diseases. (How) are these diseases related to sex? I suggest that it is possible to think of diseases *not* as being at home in a body that is already either male or female, but rather as being elements in the sexing and subjection of bodies (Harding, 1993).

Historical research has been important in deconstructing notions of the sexed body by showing that it is a variable idea in history and the product of cultural and economic relations of the time (Laqueur, 1990; Martin, 1989). (This is discussed in Chapter 3.) However, this research does not illuminate the specific ways in which the sexualised body is *produced* and its effects in the present. Nor does it directly help to open up diverse positions from which to speak as mothers – that is, reveal the figure of mother as constituted through a variety of practices of femininity, which in turn has implications for subjects positioned as men and practices of masculinity.

From a Foucauldian and many feminist perspectives, the production of medical knowledge about women's bodies and their sexualities involves the exercise of power. Medical accounts of women's bodies do not constitute a neutral act of description, rather they are acts of creation, analysis, assessment and diagnosis which in turn occasion interventions designed to treat and correct. Medical discourse is concerned with control and regulation and is one of a number of discourses (including law and social science) which bring into being and focuses on 'a problematic feminine subject who is constantly in need of surveillance and regulation' (Smart, 1992: 7). Disruption and unruliness are in turn seen 'to stem from the very biology of the body of Woman' (ibid.). New reproductive technologies appear to occasion a new round of interventions, which turn out to be not dissimilar from old ones.

New reproductive technologies and *the* sex act

How do 'new reproductive technologies' transform the (re)production of sex/uality? What does it mean if reproduction is divorced from *the* sex act (heterosexual intercourse)?

Artificial contraception (mechanical, chemical, surgical) and homosexuality, of course, have effected the historic divorce of sexuality from reproduction – producing sex without reproduction. New reproductive technologies (NRTs) offer the converse – reproduction without sex. NRTs are deployed where sexual activity fails to produce a pregnancy. Technologically assisted reproduction without sex opens up the possibility of differently configured cultural relations: families consisting of older parents, single parents and same sex parents. At the same time, political, social and economic considerations may be deployed to limit access to NRTs and so stifle new configurations of 'family'. Indeed, the deployment of NRTs may function to preserve the conventional heterosexual nuclear family. In this sense, although reproduction occurs (or not) in the absence of penetrative hetero-sex, NRTs help to reproduce (the hegemony of) *the* sex act.

The deployment of new reproductive technologies reinforces the idea that reproduction is a crucial ingredient of normal sex – being a woman or a man – and that this is essentially a biological function. Other forms of parenting – adoption, being part of an extended co-parenting network – are effectively disavowed. Childrearing is redefined as the private activity of the heterosexual couple, located in the domestic sphere, despite being rerouted through the clinic (a semi-private/public space) and the couple being 'outed' as infertile.

This version of sexuality as heterosexual and reproductive is sustained even when some of the biological bits are not the couple's own. Adele Clarke's distinction between modern and postmodern approaches to reproductive bodies and processes is useful here. Modern approaches, Clarke argues, were and remain based on 'achieving and/or enhancing *control* over [those] bodies and processes', whereas postmodern approaches are centred on 're/de/sign and *transformation of* reproductive bodies and processes to achieve a variety of goals' (Clarke, 1995: 140). However, representation of and intervention in these bodily processes remains highly contested. Modern approaches have not disappeared with the advent of postmodern ones; rather, they coexist.

According to Clarke, modernisation is concerned with extending control over an increasing range of the environment as part of the ideology of 'science as progress'. Modern control over reproductive processes is achieved through industrialisation (Clarke, 1995: 141). Modern industrialisation involves 'rationalisation (segmentation of a larger process into smaller sub-parts more amenable to manipulation), standardisation, efficiency, planning, specialisation, professionalisation, commodity and technological development, and profitability' (ibid.: 142–3). This involves the development and mass production of new consumer goods (like commercial menstrual products) and new technologies (like hormones, contraceptives, pharmaceuticals) and the organisation and mass distribution of basic reproductive services including obstetrics and 'family planning'. Modern approaches to reproductive processes are distinguished by 'universalising tendencies' and a focus on sameness – 'they were and remain aimed at the masses while they operate, for the most part , in/on individual women's bodies' (ibid.: 143). These approaches focus on specific processes: childbirth, menstruation, pregnancy, menopause, contraception and abortion.

In modernity, the lived individual body is to be planned and changes are to be controlled across the life span. At the level of the social body, a naturalised heterosexual nuclear family is to be created and maintained via rational management, involving smaller and planned families by means of dissociating sex from reproduction via contraception. At the level of the body politic, population is to be controlled via contraception and enhanced legitimation and legalisation of intervention in reproductive processes. Thus, Clarke argues, (hetero)sexuality was/is assumed to be 'ubiquitous and, quite radically, was NOT to be the focus of control'. Heterosexuality was/is compulsory. Sex did/does not have to be resisted; rather, specific consequences of sexuality are to be controlled – pregnancy and sexually transmitted diseases (Clarke, 1995: 144–5).

In postmodernity, according to Clarke, attention is focused on transformations of the body and difference. Whereas modern approaches are aimed at controlling and limiting the quantity of children, postmodern approaches to reproductive processes offer quality control. In postmodern approaches, 'the reproductive body is transformed by customising, tailoring, re/de/sign/ing' (Clarke, 1995: 145). This involves an elaboration of specific services (infertility services, sex preselection services, genetic screening, foetal screening, treatments and surgeries) which are (re)organised for selectively targeted delivery (usually individuals and families, who can afford them) (ibid.).

Postmodernist approaches focus on assisted conception and infertility treatments involving NRTs. NRTs are high tech, cutting edge medicine, unlike services aimed at prevention of infertility (sex education, STD education, birth control education, etc.). NRTs sustain the nineteenth-century concern to ensure that upper- and middle-class women do have children, because NRTs are expensive and so only available to the wealthy. Pregnancy is the focus of a wide array of new surveillance technologies in postmodernity, 'including fetal surveillance related to potential surgical interventions *in utero*' (Clarke, 1995: 146). Women are being disembodied and pregnant women's bodies are being made peripheral to the real subject, the foetus. (This issue is discussed in more detail in Chapter 3.) Additionally, male reproductive phenomena are being increasingly studied.

The lived reproductive body, in postmodernity, is tailored to fit fashion and possible (re)constructions of 'family' with the help of reproductive technologies. This body is neither stable nor singular: it is a cyborg. Cyborgs can accumulate desired characteristics and capacities and delete undesired ones. One postmodern goal is the transformation of 'the currently lived body into the desired lived body aligned with a desired social body'. In turn, the social body can be reconstructed many times 'with new meanings for mother, father, and family (biological/ social/ surrogate/ donor/ other)' (Clarke, 1995: 147–8).

> Postmodern familial design capacities allow a new disaggregation. If in the modern framework, heterosexuality could be set free from its reproductive consequences, in the postmodern frame, gender, sex and sexuality can all be disaggregated from reproduction. (ibid.: 148)

Postmodernity appears to offer infinite transformative possibilities. NRTs have the capacity to transform ideas of 'what it is to be human, male, female, reproductive, parent, child, fetus, family, race and even population' (ibid.: 149).

The transformations made possible by NRTs are not uncontested. Feminists have challenged the deconstruction, fragmentation, alienation, and consequent devaluing of motherhood as well as the commoditisation of women and children entailed in postmodern approaches to reproduction (Stanworth, 1987). Right-wing politicians, moral campaigners and journalists have contested reconstructions of the family and, as part of this, have generated a public discourse vilifying single mothers and lesbian mothers.

The transformative capacities of NRTs – including the disaggregation of sex, gender and sexuality from reproduction and the reconstruction of families – are themselves limited by social, economic and political factors which condition access to NRTs. This certainly includes wealth, but may also include (in the UK, at least) sexual orientation, marriage and age. Technologies are not autonomous; they are deployed from specific institutional sites, within existing discourses and the relations of power/ knowledge they support. How are medical experts compelled to support/ refuse new configurations of the family?

New reproductive technologies also function to nominate 'ideal reproducers'. The customisation of bodies and targeting of individual consumers is accompanied by a distinct (modernist) message about who cannot and should not reproduce. The various ways in which sexuality today can be articulated in relation to fertility reveal persistent tensions between modern and postmodern approaches to reproduction. In the rest of this chapter, I look closely at the questions raised by 'older' women seeking to become mothers and the donation and procurement of ova. In the next chapter, I explore the positioning of teenage, single and lesbian mothers as 'unfit' and publically voiced concerns about mothers' economic dependence and the absence of men from family units.

Spare parts and the 'yuck factor'

New reproductive technologies reveal the body and sex to be radically unstable and highly mutable. NRTs appear capable of creating new sex/ualities and making 'mother' connote a variety of subject positions. NRTs also function to reinforce the idea that maternity is the desire of all women.

> Science can now do (or will be able to do, if it is permitted to continue with the research) the following things: allow a 59–year-old post-menopausal woman to conceive twins; assist a black woman to give birth to a genetically white baby; and transfer the eggs of aborted fetuses to the uterus of another woman. Whether the general public wants science to do any of these things is another matter. (Grant, 1994: 6)

> The first two technological marvels occurred without public discussion, whereas the last was the subject of a public consultation exercise (ibid.).

In 1993, the Human Fertility and Embryology Authority (HFEA) published a consultation document aimed at stimulating 'public debate' about the 'legal, scientific, social, ethical and moral issues and implications' of new research in the field of reproductive technology (HFEA, 1993: 1).[2] The HFEA was considering whether to license research and fertility treatment involving the use of 'ovarian tissue obtained from mature women, from girls or women who have died (cadaveric tissue), or from aborted fetuses' and was concerned that 'the public' might be revolted by such bodily transformations:

> The HFEA is aware that while the public is generally willing to accept organ donation and the use of fetal tissue for therapeutic purposes generally, it may feel an instinctive repugnance to the use of ovarian tissue from these sources for research or fertility treatment. The HFE Act has resolved the earlier debate on research on human embryos, but the public may still be alarmed that the frontiers of medical science are being pushed forward too far and too fast. The Authority has a role in informing the public about these issues in a balanced way. (HFEA, 1993: 2)

In the print media, repugnance was taken for granted and dubbed 'the yuck factor'. What seemed most 'abject', in Kristeva's sense of the term (Kristeva, 1982), was the use of cadavers and aborted foetuses as the source of donated body parts. This particular postmodern manipulation promised to erode a boundary separating life and death and, in the case of the aborted foetus especially, confuse the meanings of life and death.

The use of donated ova and sperm precipitates questions about 'identity' – especially, where individual identity, lived within the heterosexual nuclear family, is inscribed through a biological/genetic discourse. For an individual born by a result of assisted conception, the following questions may arise: who is my father (in the case of donated sperm)? who is my 'genetic' mother (in the case of donated ova)? or even, what if my 'genetic' mother died as a child (in the case of cadaveric tissue) or never lived outside of the womb (in the case of foetal tissue)? In the latter case, a generation would be skipped and conventional familial relations would be disrupted. Would the child who is born seek out its 'grandparents' and ask why they killed its mother?

Foetal tissue is already used for research into disease but not to produce other foetuses. The latter use also raises questions of ownership and consent. Informed consent sounds very well but what rights does it confer, especially with regard to relationship to children produced (mother/grandmother/ grandfather)?

In the HFEA document, and media discussion of it, concerns are expressed about the 'effects' on children of the circumstances of their conception. In this discussion, a need for information about one's own genetic background is formulated as a right or condition of normal subjecthood.[3] This reflects a cultural imperative for each individual to be able to relate a 'narrative of self' using the concepts and language of biological/genetic discourse. The transgression and manipulation of bodily borders is also confusing cultural relations inscribed on them and which they (bodily borders) reinforce, support and naturalise.

The HFEA and media texts express anxieties about possible abnormalities in babies born as a result of 'skipping a generation'.

> Ovarian tissue or eggs from an aborted fetus have not been subjected to the pressures which govern survival and normal development to adulthood. This raises questions about the degree of risk of abnormality, at present unquantifiable, in embryos produced using such tissue. This might be seen as breaking a natural law of biology. (HFEA, 1993: 6)

A discourse on evolution is in play here which 'naturalises' the relations of the heterosexual nuclear family as a social and reproductive unit. It also insists that reproduction means the production of normal healthy babies for the right sort of patients.

Medical experts, the HFEA document claims, are constrained in their efforts to help heterosexual couples reproduce by a shortage of eggs caused by wastage and lack of supply. According to the HFEA public consultation document, demand for donated ova outweighs supply. Insufficient women come forward to donate ova. The HFEA report reflects that age may be a factor contributing to demand for donated ova. Ova donation procedures may be the only option for older women who want to conceive but do not produce sufficient quality and quantity of ova – either because they never produced enough or because they delayed maternity (for the sake of their careers). According to the HFEA, the methods used to obtain mature eggs are seen as partly to blame for the shortage, since they involve adult women in 'intrusive and uncomfortable medical procedures which are not without risk' and taking drugs 'to stimulate the production of several mature eggs' (HFEA, 1993: 3). As Linda Grant suggested in the *Guardian* 'no amount of publicity about what is involved in donation is likely to increase the number of volunteers' (1994: 7):

First, menopause is artificially induced, then the cycle is restarted and daily doses of a drug called FSH (Follicle Stimulating Hormone) are given. Instead of producing a single egg, large numbers appear and are harvested by a probe and needle into the vagina. The chemical interference, the discomfort, the knowledge that possibly many children are walking around who are genetically related to the donor, all combine to make egg donation a major commitment, in no way analogous to sperm donation with its curtained cubicles and piles of *Playboy*. (ibid.)

The enormous physical, emotional and cultural cost of 'the gift' – ova donation – prefigures the significance of using new, dead donors. The advantages of using 'donated adult cadaveric or fetal ovarian tissue', it is argued, are that they could 'provide many more eggs for IVF and embryo research than are currently available'. Indeed 'there are millions of immature eggs in foetal ovaries and thousands still remaining in the normally fertile adult woman which have the potential to ripen into mature eggs' (HFEA, 1993: 4). The female body is thus inscribed as a repository of (lost) reproductive potential.

Who would donate ova? Current donors may be women undergoing sterilisation who are prepared to donate eggs, or women who have surplus eggs after fertility treatment. Donors may be friends or relatives of a recipient but 'usually women donate anonymously simply because they wish to help other women who are infertile' (HFEA, 1993: 3).

This text helps to produce an image of women united in their desire for maternity. Pregnancy, and the delivery of a normal healthy baby, is perceived as so acutely part of sex/uality that some women will undergo painful procedures to help other women whom they will never meet achieve it. This medically constructed and mediated sorority is based on the export/import of body parts. But what pressures are women already having treatment under? It is not possible to know from the information presented, but they are likely to be in a vulnerable position. This is all part of the production of a socially desired body – pregnant and able to deliver a perfect healthy baby.

Implicit in discussion about NRTs is the idea that, in postmodernity, you can have everything (as long as you are wealthy enough). You can delay childbearing until you are socially, emotionally and financially secure. This reflects middle-class values and ideals regarding the material and social conditions of reproduction and childrearing. It also proposes this as an 'appropriate' and desirable performance of motherhood. The mother figured here is one who makes choices – she chooses to delay childbearing, uses technologies to assist conception if she needs them, undergoes pre-natal screening and interventions, aborts abnormal foetuses which cannot be operated on. The mother figured is to be congratulated, since these choices pay off – the child is perfect and healthy, much longed for and is welcomed into a loving conventional, financially secure family unit.

But how are women as mothers positioned in this? When ova are donated and a pregnancy ensues, women gestate and deliver a baby, but they do not pass on their own genetic material. Their male partners passing on their genes. Adoption has been foreclosed – perhaps by a lack of babies for adoption, perhaps by the couple's age, perhaps by the desire of the male partner to be a genetic parent. The bodily grounds for female reproductive sexuality will have to be (re)constructed in terms of pregnancy and birth (away from genes).

The investment (time and money) in this (often less than reliable) technology underlines the importance of parenthood for contemporary gendered identity and its expression as sexuality. It is an option most easily available to those who can afford it. My discussion is not intended to be anti-technology. Rather, I want to show how the use of these technologies (within existing discourses and institutional contexts) helps to produce sex/ualities. My premise is that technology is not introduced into and does not impact on pre-formed nature and social contexts but is an integral part of them – constituted in and constitutive of them. Technology is neither autonomous nor purely instrumental.

Older women exercising 'choice' and control over their lives are constituted and targeted as the main consumers of NRTs. However, it seems that older women occupy an ambiguous 'highly qualified' subject position. How 'old' can 'older' be? For example, there has been substantial public criticism of women over 50 years old who undergo fertility treatments and of the particular case of a 59-year-old woman who gave birth to twins after receiving donated ova.

Public discussion about who is fit to be a mother

Ova donation extends the age at which women can be mothers and helps to make maternity the desire of women, even into their forties. However, journalists and scientists appear to draw the line at 50.

A leading article in the *Independent* (21 July 1993: 21) describes the controversial work of Severino Antinori, an Italian gynaecologist, in helping a 58-year-old British woman to become pregnant with twins. The journalist poses the question: 'should doctors routinely refuse fertility treatment to older women?'. Since it is mainly paid for by individuals, the issue is less one of public policy and more a question of ethics and practicality. Some women, it is argued, 'are so desperate to have children that they will continue to pay for treatment year after year, hoping against hope that the doctor may enable them to give birth'. In deciding whether to help these women, specialists must consider whether, ethically, 'there is anything wrong or unnatural in helping women to defeat the processes that render them infertile as they become older'. If they decide to help them, where should the line be drawn? More women are choosing to postpone childbearing until after they have worked for some years. This may not be such a bad thing if it helps them 'better to love and support their children'. The practical reasons to think twice about fertility treatments for older women are that there is a shortage of eggs, and because of this, doctors should consider the welfare of the child that will be born 'before implanting those scarce eggs into older women'.

> A mother in her mid-fifties may find it hard to get up in the night to feed her baby; five years on, her physique may be unable to take the strain of scrabbling around the floor with her toddler. There is also the greater risk of turning a child into an orphan if its parents are septuagenarians before it reaches its teens (*Independent*, 21 July 1993: 21).

The article concludes by saying that 'good mothers can be over 50, just as bad mothers can be under 20'. 'Common sense' suggests that doctors should be sceptical of older women who want to bear children but 'they should resist attempts to impose a firm age limit; and treat each case with the sympathy and dignity it deserves' (ibid.).

A further article, in the same edition of the *Independent*, reported that 'thirteen women over the age of 50 have been treated in British clinics since 1991 to help them become pregnant' and two have succeeded in having babies. The chairman of the Human Fertilisation and Embryology Authority was quoted as saying that the authority was uneasy about assisting post-menopausal women and that the public was concerned that children of 10 years old might be severely disadvantaged by having mothers of 70 (*Independent*, 21 July 1993: 3). Children should be able to expect their parents to be 'young enough', meaning able-bodied enough, 'to play football in the park with them', which is part of growing up in a normal family (Winston, 1993).

Robert Winston (professor of fertility studies at Hammersmith Hospital, London) writing in the *Guardian* argued 'the limits of fertility are being stretched too far in allowing middle-aged women to become mothers' (Winston, 1993). Winston stated that any pregnancy in a woman in her late fifties or early sixties carries considerable risks to her health, and a twin pregnancy, after transfer of several embryos, seems even more fraught:

> Whilst pregnancy in the forties is now commonplace and easily managed, once a woman gets much beyond the age of fifty, virtually all the serious complications of pregnancy are much more likely. High blood pressure, toxaemia of pregnancy, heart disease, diabetes, and thrombosis are all relatively probable and she is less likely to have the strength for her newborn in the event of its safe delivery. (Winston, 1993)

He goes on to say that there is a significant chance that a woman might miscarry at any stage in her pregnancy and whilst this is always a shattering event for anyone, it may be especially devastating for an older woman:

this group of older women are particularly vulnerable to suffer extraordinary psychological trauma. The few women who actually seek such treatment in their later years are often desperate people, sometimes quite disturbed emotionally. (ibid.)

Winston addresses (what he sees as) the concerns, at a personal level, of women donating ova, and, at a public level, of 'ordinary people and our political representatives'. Ova donors undergo 'complex and demanding treatment' from which they can derive 'no personal benefit' and their feelings should be considered:

> I have spoken to hundreds of potential egg donors and all of them say they are horrified at the mere thought that their own genetic children might be given away to women 20 years older than themselves. (ibid.)

Winston distinguishes a deserving group of recipients – 'women who have suffered a premature menopause as a result of a pathological event' – from an undeserving group who wish 'to use high technology to subvert a natural, biological event'. The latter group are accused of debasing 'the value of menopause, when our energies and experience may be better spent in more mature activities'. Winston is concerned that the activities of Dr Antinori and the publicity which surrounds them, in enabling a 59-year-old woman to give birth, 'risk bringing a highly valuable and vulnerable technology into public disrepute'. The public, he argues, already worry that through the deployment of NRTs 'doctors and scientists are tampering with the very elements of human life'. It is important for practitioners of IVF to be sensitive to 'the worries of ordinary people and our political representatives' or 'risk jeopardising the whole funding and future of proper reproductive medicine'.[4]

These texts address a target audience of customers for IVF who are in their forties but not in their fifties. The transformation of individual bodies to fit the socially desired body is delimited by age. Despite the extensive manipulation of bodily borders involved in the deployment of NRTs, the term 'natural' has some currency in this discourse. It describes desiring children when referring to women in their forties, and not desiring children when referring to women in their fifties. Women in their fifties who seek assisted conception are positioned as desperate, unnatural, and a cause of physical and psychological suffering to any children born.

What is wrong with cyborgs and with 'designer babies' and 'designer families'? Women seeking assisted conception may put forward the 'pro-choice argument', insisting that it is a 'private matter between a woman and her doctor' – 'a woman's right to choose' (Grant, 1994: 7).[5] However, 'choice' has been shown to be the historical product of a discourse on liberal individualism – focused on the basic tenets of choice, privacy and rights – which is increasingly seen as problematic (Himmelweit, 1988; Poovey, 1992) because it presumes (and, therefore, constitutes) a notion of 'personhood' which is bound to sets of (uneven) assumptions about gender and race in which women and black people are homogenised and subordinated. 'Choice' is an individualising, privatising construct deployed by right and left, in conservative and radical projects. 'Choice' has politically different meanings in different political contexts. A black woman, with a white husband, chose to have a donated egg from a white woman to ensure that her child would be white and not be subjected to the racism she encountered herself. As Grant points out, this is 'problematic since it has a political context beyond the social and scientific' (Grant, 1994: 8). It has the stench of eugenics: 'even though the woman has made the choice, it was a choice made in a racist society' (ibid.). On the other hand, does public distaste for this bodily transformation (making the lived body consistent with the desired social body) reflect the racism of those who do not like the idea of a white baby being brought up by a black mother? Again, does this echo nineteenth-century obsessions with racial purity (Gordon, 1977; Grant, 1994; Weeks, 1989)? Indeed, 'there's a frisson that comes with an appreciation of the radical mutability of the body' (Grant, 1994: 8).

Why do women want children? Or why are they being positioned as desperate to have children through these media/medical/ethical discourses? Why do some women not want children and others spend thousands and endure pain to get them? What about preventing infertility?

Use of donated ova, together with 'the yuck factor', exemplifies postmodern concern with manipulation and customisation and with targeting special consumer groups. It is concerned with difference, rather than sameness, but difference is also carefully circumscribed and controlled. New freedoms (so-called) bring with them new and not so new controls and limitations. Gendered subjects are interpellated to enact gender and be mothers in precise ways. In the next chapter I examine the ways in which sex/uality is controlled through (resistances to) the creation of 'queer families'.

Notes

1. Martin interviewed women about their 'experiences' of bodily processes to elicit possible alternative visions. In women's descriptions, menstrual blood is unclean and signifies death, disease or injury, as well as defining one as a woman and able to have a baby.

2. The role of the HFEA is outlined in the document. The HFEA was set up by the 1990 Human Fertility and Embryology Act (the HFE Act) which is 'concerned with regulating the provision of certain fertility treatments and any research involving human embryos' (HFEA, 1993: 1). The HFEA licenses 67 IVF clinics in Britain and exists to regulate, via a licensing system, all centres in the UK carrying out: (a) fertility treatment which involves the use of donated eggs or sperm (e.g. donor insemination), or of embryos created outside of the body (*in vitro* fertilisation or IVF); (b) storage of eggs, sperm and embryos; and, (c) research using human embryos.

3. The need for information about one's own genetic background is increasingly being required as a precondition for married reproduction or for those who have already miscarried foetuses where investigation (on those used in research and treatment) reveals a genetically inherited condition (where this then becomes a source of information for those who produced the aborted and donated foetus).

4. 'IVF is already a relatively privileged treatment, heavily rationed by ailing health services throughout the Western world' (Winston, 1993).

5. Public discussion of NRTs and the 'yuck factor' has the potential for reopening debate on abortion. The logic put forward is 'If you use technology to control one, you must allow it to assist the other' (Grant, 1994: 8).

8

QUEER FAMILIES

The subversive potential of cyborgs

The reproductive body has become a cyborg, capable of jettisoning unde-sirable characteristics and accumulating desired ones (Clarke, 1995). Conception may occur apart from heterosexual intercourse. Postmodern approaches to reproduction provoke discontinuities between the sexed body, gender and sexuality and enable potentially subversive perfor-mances of gender. This opens up possibilities for new choices and reconstructions of 'the family'. These possibilities are in turn played out within the constraints exercised through existing discourses which con-verge to define and position the figure of mother and make it an exemplary practice of femininity. Such constraints are most evident where new choices and discontinuities in sex/uality are problematised. An examina-tion of the definition of some sex/ualities as 'troubling' reveals some of the detailed ways in which motherhood is produced as a gendered perfor-mance (including a stipulation of what it should and should not include).

The limits placed on the potential of postmodern approaches to radically re-create modern families (by stressing individual choice and possibilities for constructing a desired body) are evident from public discussion of lesbian and teenage mothers. Sexuality is problematised in the public gaze by virtue of its consequences and contexts, political, moral and economic.

In this chapter I am concerned with aspects of political and moral dis-course as they interpellate sexual subjects in the 1990s to position mothers as suitable or unsuitable, to celebrate some gendered performances and to condemn others. I examine the tensions within a political discourse which emphasises 'choice', individuals' rights to customise lifestyles (if they can afford it), the traditional heterosexual nuclear family unit and the impor-tance to children and society of fathers. I look at the ways in which the public gaze has focused on mothers (teenage and lesbian) who deviate from this model family and disrupt heterosexuality.

Income is a significant factor and influences the ways in which the sub-ject position of mother is culturally and politically inflected. More especially it influences whether it will be paraded in public and publicly dissected and judged. 'Economic dependence' is what makes single, teenage and some lesbian mothers into sexual deviants. At the same time, economic dependence has traditionally defined the (culturally revered) married heterosexual mother who stays at home looking after children.

Maternity as difference

Motherhood, as a practice of femininity, is persistently produced through various discourses, spoken from different institutional sites, as a way of understanding the materiality of the body which underpins and confirms hetero-sex/uality and grounds it in biology. Biological discourse produces maternity as a process which includes all women (potentially and actually) in a seamless category of sameness. But the lived experience of motherhood intersects with many other lived experiences and subject positions (shaped by the uneven relations of class, race, disability and age, for example). Motherhood, as a practice of femininity and performance of gender, is variable – it takes place in different (social, economic and ethnic) contexts and is 'subject to social, economic and cultural practices and systems' (Woodward, 1997: 240). Our understandings of motherhood are formed through representations which indicate 'what constitutes good or bad mothering' and, even, those 'for whom motherhood is or is not appropriate' (ibid.). But maternity might be achieved through various different routes (sexual intercourse, artificial insemination, *in vitro* fertilisation, adoption or step-parenting) and might intersect with other subject positions.

> Mothers can be lesbian, heterosexual, married, single or divorced, where each of these subject-positions can be differently inflected and culturally defined' (ibid.).

Some of these subject positions are defined as troublesome. Recently, public attention has been drawn to the phenomena of 'lesbian mums'. The print media have again provided a forum in which certain views can be aired and discourses on motherhood played out. My attention was grabbed by the *Sun*'s headlines:

LESBIANS PAY £5 FOR A BABY. Fury at DIY pregnancy (29 April 1997: 1)

Gay mums are making a sickening mockery of motherhood (13 May 1997: 4)

These headlines and the subsequent stories are a useful focus for discussion of the constraints operating to define and position the figure of mother, not because they are necessarily true or false, nor because they represent a majority view (they may or they may not, we do not know). Indeed, other newspapers have carried similar stories and the angle has varied somewhat. It is not necessary to take what is published in the *Sun* as fact or to dismiss it is as bawdy fiction. Newspapers, like the media in general, are not autonomous: they are institutional sites from which discourses already in play are spoken. So, what is said in the *Sun* (which, after all is bought by 10 million UK newspaper readers) resonates with and reproduces elements of discourses spoken elsewhere. A detailed consideration of what exactly is troubling about the sex/ualities described will help to reveal some of the ways in which discourse impels gendered performances and constructs 'the figure of mother' (Woodward, 1997: 225).

The images of lesbians produced through this particular sexual exposure have been very different to that generated by media interest in 'lesbian chic'. Instead of being represented as glamorous, attractive and expensively dressed, the lesbian mothers featured in the *Sun* appear 'downmarket' and anything but 'chic'. Butch/femme roles, sexual histories, method of conception and dependence on welfare benefits are constituted as objects of comment – that is, analysis and judgement.

The articles constitute sites for the enunciation of distinctive discourses on sexuality (identifying married heterosexuality as the norm and everything else as deviant); gender (indicating the appearance of normal femininity by drawing attention to deviations from it, like cropped hair, and identifying butch and femme roles in each of the lesbian couples discussed); morality (focusing on the rights of children and the responsibilities and irresponsibilities of parenthood); and economy (emphasising the cost of bringing up a child and the dependence of the women discussed on state benefits). Fathers figure in both moral and economic discourses as an absence which will deprive children of a normal upbringing and leave the state to pay the bills.

There are several routes to lesbian motherhood. Some women choose same sex partners after having had children. Some women choose same sex partners and later decide that they would also like to have children, in which case they may seek conception using donor insemination. Donor insemination (using the sperm of an anonymous donor) has been widely practised in fertility clinics for a long time to enable women to conceive when their male partner has been diagnosed as infertile. In this circumstance, donor insemination is not often publicly discussed or problematised (except in relation to men's feelings about infertility and the acceptability to them of parenting children who are not 'biologically theirs'). The donor's identity is protected by law. Donor insemination appears to be a very different issue where lesbians are concerned. It is affected by economic considerations and is made a matter of public concern, when the parties involved are jobless and poor. In this circumstance, pressure is exerted on women to disclose the identity of the donor (unprotected by law in this instance).

Lesbians may seek donor insemination in medically controlled clinics, if they can afford it, and may or may not be allowed access to this technology if they are 'out' about being lesbians. They may pose as straight single women, if clinics are prepared to 'treat' single women (and many are not).

The availability of donor insemination in clinics to declared lesbian and single women is influenced by social, moral and political discourse which presumes to define what constitutes the 'proper family' and 'the best interests of the child', and makes the presence of a male partner and 'father' central to both of these.

Lesbians may organise insemination by donor for themselves, possibly through friendship/other social networks or through advertising, and negotiate subsequent relations with the donor (after conception and birth). This appears to be a private arrangement (though public channels of communication may be used) and it remains so until various moments of 'coming out' are negotiated: telling other family members of the pregnancy; dealing with health professionals during pregnancy and birth; setting up child-care arrangements. For those who are on benefits the arrangement is potentially much less private. Self-insemination becomes a matter of public concern, and vilification, when highlighted by the press and when individual lesbian couples (not even single parents) refuse to name the friend who helped them have a child and are claiming state benefits.

As a postmodern approach to reproduction, lesbian self-insemination is very 'low tech'. It is also low cost. Women do not have to be wealthy to purchase this service – they may organise and carry it out for themselves. In a sense, they have taken conception into their own hands and are (for a while at least) in control of the process. This taking of control is subject to scrutiny within a moral discourse which draws attention to the fact that they have 'done it themselves' and accuses them of being 'selfish'.

Scandal of Britain's most selfish mums: LESBIAN LOVERS HAVE A DIY BABY EACH (*Sun*, 13 May 1997: 1)

To have done it once is bad enough; to do it again is much worse. One of the women is pregnant and the other already has a child. The moral discourse articulated through the text emphasises the 'normal' composition of the family as heterosexual. The women are accused of creating a family which is not normal and not acceptable, most especially because it is perceived to exclude the figure of father. The caption beneath the accompanying photograph of the two women and a baby reads:

> *Flawed family . . . lesbian Lisa with her baby daughter Terri and pregnant lover Dawn, right*

Readers are informed that the women had become pregnant using the sperm of different male friends. Dawn, 21, got pregnant by impregnating herself with sperm collected in a 'pickled onion jar', and has been 'slammed' by politicians and pro-family campaigners 'for bringing children into the world without fathers' (*Sun*, 13 May 1997: 4). The views expressed are that children need fathers, and that it is selfish and self-indulgent for women to have children without male partners who are prepared to be fathers. They are accused of not considering the need of the child to grow up in a household its peers will find acceptable. The view is also expressed that there is injustice in a lesbian having children when other – respectable married heterosexual – women cannot and that this sickens some people.

Whilst the text focuses on the absence of a father, it also puts in question the presence of a suitable (and conventional) mother figure. The reader is 'orientated' by the fact that 'both girls posed in their Manchester United shirts' and left to ponder the inference that the child born fatherless might be further disadvantaged by an apparent disregard for 'normal' feminine attire and deportment.

An economic discourse is articulated through the text's focus on the fact that the pair are currently jobless and 'the £215-per-week cost of the bizarre family will be footed by the taxpayer'. A spokesman for the Child Support Agency is quoted as saying that unless they name the fathers of their children their benefits could be cut by 40 per cent (*Sun*, 13 May 1997: 5). The adjective 'bizarre' implies that Lisa and Dawn's family is highly idiosyncratic, very unusual and almost unthinkable, thereby downplaying any perceived threat to the cultural hegemony of the normal heterosexual family unit.

The other 'facts' which are assumed to concern the *Sun* reading public are the sexual histories of the pair (one was married to an RAF sergeant but later divorced him, the other has never had sex with a man and is the butch side of the relationship). These statements are part of a discourse constituting heterosexuality. That is, they reposition the women within a regime of heterosexuality and the gender roles it compels, to imply that lesbianism is no more than a (very poor) copy of heterosexuality. The text implies that this is confirmed by Dawn's statements

'I have known I was a lesbian since the age of 11.'

'Lisa is the feminine side of the relationship and I am butch. So I have to be a father figure, especially if my baby is a boy.'

'I hope it's a boy.'

On the one hand, this statement is highly conservative. Dawn's gender performance appears fully circumscribed by the binary frame of gender. On the other hand, there is a discontinuity between the sexed body which is assumed and the gender that is enacted, and Dawn's statement can be read as assuming that the social role of father (though part of the binary frame) is an empty space which anyone (regardless of sex/uality) could fill. The idea that Dawn, as the butch, is copying a man implies a relation of 'imitation' and 'original' which Judith Butler's performative theory of gender calls into question. For Butler, there is no original or authentic gender which can be copied, since gender is not an attribute but an act which is all imitation and parody (see Chapter 4). Dawn is imitating specific versions of gender, as are subjects constituted as men (and women).

Dawn and Lisa are accused 'of making a mockery of motherhood by having DIY babies'. It is clear that their family disaggregates sex, gender and sexuality and that this undermines motherhood as it is defined through prevailing contemporary discourses.

Support for the women came from Lisa's step-mum who said: 'Apart from being lesbians, they are ordinary people, not weirdos' (*Sun*, 13 May 1997: 4). Dawn's mother asserts that they appear to have a stable relationship, are excellent with the baby and that Dawn is the best daughter that anyone could have. They go on to claim that they are as capable of bringing up a family as anyone. Again, it appears that the subject positions of good parent/mother/father may be filled by anyone, whatever the discontinuities embodied in their sex/uality. However, Dawn appears to reinscribe sexuality within the most limited bounds of heterosexuality, and in the same gesture further pathologises her own (assumed) sexual practice, by saying

'We are not going to bring our children up to be gay, so what's the problem? We want our kids to grow up well balanced. We want Terri to go out with boys. And if I have a son, he'll go out with girls.' (*Sun*, 13 May 1997: 5)

Of course, the reader does not know what the women interviewed actually said and how this has been crafted into the printed text by journalist and editor. It is not clear how they came to speak so publically about this private arrangement, and allow themselves to be photographed (no attempt has been made to disguise the identities of either couple or their child), especially since it may have severe financial consequences for them.

The economic and moral concerns aroused by this new family are linked by the *Sun*'s 'agony aunt' who concedes that, had the women been able to pay for treatment we would probably have heard nothing of it. If they had well paid professional jobs, this would be a private affair. It would not have been brought to public attention and would not have become troublesome and outrageous.

Cultural hegemony is asserted through the text by its use of disparaging terms like 'flawed' and 'bizarre' to describe this redesigned family – thereby pathologising and individualising, removing it from its wider political and social contexts (including other forms of difference and discontinuities in the subject position 'father').

Another *Sun* article focused on the economic aspects of another 'queer family'.

A JOBLESS lesbian couple sparked a fury last night by having a DIY baby after placing a £5 advert for a sperm donor.

Crop-haired Rachel Henshaw, 24, gave birth to daughter Chloe after a gay Brazilian student answered their plea. (29 April 1997: 1)

The arrangement was branded an 'absolute disgrace' by politicians and child-support groups.
The lesbians pick up £220 a week in state benefits – and four month old Chloe's father will contribute nothing. (ibid.: 4)

Rachel is quoted as insisting 'we have done nothing wrong. We desperately wanted a baby. We are a perfect family.' She asserts that the family is first and foremost a place of caring, where two parents lovingly bring up children. This may occur regardless of the parents' sex. In this way, she reinvents the perfect nuclear family as queer.

The couple had been refused artificial insemination at NHS clinics because they are lesbians. And they could not afford to have private treatment. (ibid.)

Moral crusaders insist that women who reject men (the assumed logic of lesbianism) should not expect to have children, thereby reinscribing maternity as the proper effect and confirmation of heterosexuality. Again the women are accused of being selfish and ignoring the problems that the child will encounter. A Conservative MP is quoted as saying that a child needs a mother and a father, not two mums. He asks who is going to pay to bring up the child. Again, the Child Support Agency is quoted as saying that the women may have to pay back some of their benefits unless they name the father.

Public discourse on lesbian mothers brings sex and mothers together in particular ways. Lesbian mothers represent an alternative construction of mother and ambiguity in enactments of sex. Public discourse on lesbian mums incorporates a biological discourse which naturalises the maternal body and makes it 'the law of women's desire'. This discourse produces an original sexed body which gives rise to motherhood as a particular gendered performance and interpretation of it (the body). Motherhood is constituted as natural for women, but only as the result of heterosexuality expressed within marriage. Moral and political discourses focus on and condemn the 'unnatural' expression of sex/uality in lesbian motherhood. Lesbian mothers are, on the one hand, natural and, on the other, unnatural, selfish and immoral. They are constructed as a danger to their children and to society.

Moral and political discourses on motherhood

Conservative political discourse articulated in the 1980s and 1990s, according to Kathryn Woodward, attempted to define and 'fix' the position of mother, limiting the meanings it might have, aligning it with marriage, monogamy, heterosexuality and staying at home to look after children (Woodward, 1997).

The economic and moral discourses of 1980s Thatcherism in the UK were central to constructions of motherhood at that time. These discourses involved a critique of 'welfare dependency' and a shift of emphasis away from 'state provision of welfare and state intervention to a reliance on the market and privatization' and 'standing on your own two feet'. The idea of the independent 'rational individual' was seen as desirable and superior (Woodward, 1997: 256–7).

> Alternatives to the married, monogamous, heterosexual mother who stays at home looking after the children were constructed as both 'unnatural' and immoral. Mothers who might show independence, whether in defining their own sexuality, earning a living or maintaining an identity separate from their children, were seen as dangerous. (Woodward, 1997: 257)

However, there was a contradiction in Thatcherism because of the emphasis on choice. Market competition is based on choice – by implication lifestyle is also a choice. There may have been attacks on deviations from traditional motherhood and even on mothers participating in the workforce, but there were no actual attempts during the 1980s to prevent them from doing so or from making lifestyle choices they could afford (Woodward, 1997: 257). This meant that single motherhood could be construed as a choice. However, if you were poor it was an unacceptable choice. Thatcherism focused on 'Victorian values' and 'the articulation of individual moral responsibility within the context of the traditional family' (Woodward, 1997: 258). The moral and political discourses of Thatcherism 'had the effect of creating outsiders, such as the "unnatural", the irresponsible or "deviant" mother, and the notion that single mothers were reproducing an underclass' (ibid.).

'The discourses of Thatcherism' constructed a dichotomy between the family and the state, in which the family represented as 'a "natural" institution' was 'set against the intrusive state which limits choice and independence' (ibid.). In these discourses, the family is represented 'as a private system of welfare and support'. Commitment to this idea persisted in the Conservative party during the 1990s and found its way into some other approaches to thinking about welfare.

'The single mother' is one figure which has featured repeatedly as a version of 'motherhood gone wrong' in the 1990s. The representation of 'the pathologised single mother' is one of the figures of motherhood constructed in contemporary political and moral discourses. Political discourse has identified single mothers as 'responsible for social problems in the wider society'. In 1993, in a House of Commons speech, Peter Lilley, the Secretary of State for Social Security, linked the 'enormity of the costs of state benefits to the demands of single mothers' (Woodward, 1997: 259). However, not all single mothers are positioned as troubling. A distinction is made between the deserving and undeserving, resonating with nineteenth-century notions of the deserving and undeserving poor. Divorced and widowed women have been viewed as deserving sympathy, not condemnation. Young teenage and working-class single mothers have been singled out for blame because they are seen as choosing to become pregnant when they are unable to support themselves and, often, as using pregnancy as a means to jump the queue for council housing.[1]

> The 'undeserving' single mother is, however, classified as a problem, a woman who acts irresponsibly and is both a drain on society's economic resources and morally reprehensible. (Woodward, 1997: 259)

This representation of 'pathologised single motherhood' produces meanings which create an identity and position women as mothers within a discourse. It is not the only one within political discourse, nor even the only one on the right. Nor are the negative representations of single motherhood confined to the political right. Other discursive constructions of motherhood, for example in popular culture, include the working mother, the caring mother and the independent mother (ibid.: 260).

Teenage sexuality

Teenage sexuality is represented as problematic in political, moral and medical discourses most especially because of its perceived consequences – notably the spread of disease, and pregnancy. Teenage pregnancy is problematised for the reasons (just discussed) that it is assumed that teenage mums will be single and dependent on welfare and produce a new generation who will also expect to be supported by the state.

Michael Adler, a medic, writes that Britain has 'the highest teenage birth rate in Western Europe' and an 'escalating incidence of sexually transmitted diseases'. As with other health issues, it is 'the socio-economically disadvantaged who have the highest morbidity in relation to sexual health'. Teenage birth rates are three times higher among manual social groups compared to non-manual (Adler, 1997: 6–7).

There has been an increase in 'the number of new cases of gonorrhea seen in sexually transmitted disease (STD) clinics in England and Wales':

> Between 1995 and 1996, there was a 17 per cent rise in males and 13 per cent in females. The greatest proportional rise was among those aged between 16 and 19 with increases of 30 per cent and 29 per cent among males and females respectively. (Adler, 1997: 6)

The target set by the last Conservative government in its document *Health of the Nation* to reduce teenage conception by 50 per cent (to a rate of 4.8 per 1,000 women) will not be met (Department of Health, 1992). Adler argues that health education and promotion have to be the way forward to better sexual health. 'Young people have a right to sound, unbiased information, which allows them to make informed choices – and they should be given that information before they start engaging in sexual intercourse' (ibid.). He argues that this has been impeded by the 1993 Education Act which 'created anomalies about sex education and contraceptive advice in schools'. He also claims that there is no evidence that school sex education will stimulate the onset of sexual experience. In addition to sex education, Adler argues, it is necessary to recognise the effects of poverty on sexual health – '"poor" sexual health can be driven by poverty and young people's sense of social alienation and worthlessness' (Adler, 1997: 6–7).[2]

This last statement is the concluding remark in Adler's article and is not elaborated. It reflects a more widely held view expressed in more liberal discourses that many working-class teenagers (who may come from various ethnic backgrounds) do have troublesome sexualities and that they deploy them in such a way as to drain society's resources. However, the argument goes, this is not entirely their fault because *they* have been failed by society. They are alienated from the economic, social and moral values of the society in which they live. They do not feel that they have a stake in society – probably because they dropped out of (or fell behind at) school. Sexuality – being sexually active and reproductive – is one way of taking up an adult subject position that confers certain benefits and status. But liberals worry about the resources (economic and social) possessed by teenage parents for bringing up children. The liberal solution to the economic burden presented by young mothers is, repeatedly, education and training.

Recently, several individual cases of teenage sex/uality were spotlighted for public attention. One article focused on 'Britain's youngest mum' and the rest, unusually, on teenage fathers.

SEX AT 11, MUM AT 12. A story to shock Britain (*Sun*, 4 July 1997: 1)

So went another front-page headline. The girl, called Jane (not her real name), was claimed to be Britain's youngest mum, having her baby a year after starting secondary school. The story goes that Jane complained of stomach ache, her mother looked under her baggy jumper to discover stretch marks, whisked her off to the GP and, a week later, she gave birth to a daughter by Caesarian section. The article describes how Jane was terrified of people's response and stayed indoors for some time after the birth. Family, neighbours and friends, and the nation, were shocked. A relative reports that 'Jane and her 13 year old boyfriend were "just experimenting" with sex when the baby was conceived . . . At 11 years old she had no idea what it would lead to. She was terrified when she found out she was pregnant – and very confused' (*Sun*, 4 July 1997: 4). The same relative asserts that Jane's mother and father have been very supportive. Jane's mother is the legal guardian of the baby. The article includes quotes from Jane about how great the baby is and how supportive her mum and dad are and from her dad about 'how difficult it has been'. Her father insists that they are a close family and do not care what others think. He is a proud grandfather (ibid.: 5). 'The 13 year old father' reportedly has 'nothing to do with the baby'. Jane will not return to school and will be allocated a home tutor and social worker. Readers are informed that the cost of home tutoring will total £22,500 per year to pay for a supply teacher and extra books and equipment.

Economic and moral discourses are, not surprisingly, at play in this article to construct a troublesome sexuality and a different, but nonetheless 'queer', family.

Jane's case produces a moral dilemma, according to the *Sun*, because although Jane and the baby are well and she has the support of her mother and the help of social services, she is too young to have sex.

> Her plight should shame and alarm us all. (*Sun*, 4 July 1997: 8)

The problem is not hers alone. She has not been adequately protected by her parents and 'society'. It is argued in the *Sun* that the legal age of consent (16 years of age) is not enforced. The law is undermined by doctors, nurses, teachers and social workers who 'listen to confessions about sex and don't tell the families' and 'advise under age children about their sex lives without being allowed to tell their parents' (ibid.: 5). These professionals are keeping sex lives private: for the best of reasons, they think they are helping. The moral crunch is that *it is not the children's fault*. They alone cannot be blamed; parents have to be responsible:

> The rest of us – her school, her family and above all her parents and all of society – must consider ourselves responsible for the loss of her innocence and her childhood. (*Sun*, 4 July 1997: 6)

A moral discourse is articulated through the assignment of blame and responsibility: how close can she and her mother have been if her mother didn't notice that her periods had started and then stopped? Who is the father? He is 'clearly someone who didn't care about leaving an 11 year old to face the music alone' (*Sun*, 4 July 1997: 6). Moral crusaders again blame lack of adequate sex education which encourages young girls to say 'no'. Others blame the entertainment industry and state provision of welfare for encouraging children to be sexually active and then helping them out when pregnancy results. 'Shame' is the antidote preferred by Conservative MP Theresa Gorman.

Writing in the *Sun*, Gorman calls for a 'return to old moral values' (5 July 1997: 5). Gorman argues that Jane's case, though sad, is not particularly surprising. She may be the youngest but there are far too many under-age pregnancies – hers is just the most disturbing: 'The trouble is a strong moral code and shame have been replaced by social services and state handouts' (ibid.). Gorman claims that

Society used to be based on families and clear rules, but now it constantly encourages sex. Kids are bombarded with sexually explicit material day and night. Virtually every TV programme, even during the day, has bonking scenes.

Teenage mags are crammed full of articles about sex and virtually encourage promiscuity.

At school, kids get sex drummed into them by well-meaning but misguided teachers.

Sex education lessons have no moral overtones and just show children how to do it.

The result is that kids know all about sex before they're hardly old enough. And many can't wait to start. (ibid.)

According to Gorman, it is 'society' that is to blame. Children need better examples from everyone. This means that 'we' must stop bombarding them with sex and helping them when things go wrong. We must stop being 'soft and sympathetic', start making people 'responsible for their behaviour' and 'stop bailing them out'.

We glorify fecklessness and there are whole neighbourhoods made up of teenage mothers living comfortably off the state. The welfare system is geared up to help those who are irresponsible and do everything for them except give them good advice.

There's an army of social workers just waiting to step in.

The state is condoning bad behaviour, instead of shaming people, and if it continues things will only get worse. (ibid.)

Reportedly these views are echoes by readers of the *Sun*.

The whole of Britain was shellshocked yesterday after reading the *Sun*'s disturbing story of a mum aged only 12.

Hundreds of readers phoned us to tell how it had worried, angered or even frightened them.

Many thought the story a grim illustration of Britain's moral decline. Some reckoned Jane's parents had questions to answer. (ibid.: 4–5)

The moral discourse articulated in the articles commenting on Jane's baby to some extent exonerates Jane, and instead points the finger of blame at those who should have protected her – 'society' (possibly made up of doctors and teachers and social workers who do not warn her off sex) and, especially, her parents. Alison Hadley of Brooke Advisory was quoted as saying that parents need to be able to discuss sex with children more honestly (ibid.: 4). Repeated reference to the responsibilities of parents is part of the Conservative/Thatcherite discourse which emphasises the traditional heterosexual nuclear family as the privatised unit of support and welfare. The 13-year-old father is also condemned for the cowardliness and lack of caring implied by his absence. His figure helps to construct under-age hetero-sex as composed of uneven and hierarchically arranged gendered desires and responsibilities. Young men fulfil their desires and disappear, leaving girls/women to 'face the music'.

> As a great debate about the issue raged across the nation, readers blamed TV shows that 'throw' sex at kids, young girls who think of babies like dolls and boys who pressurise girls into satisfying their lust. (ibid.: 4–5)

Morality crusader Victoria Gillick called for 'police to quiz the baby's father'. She said:

> If such a young girl has become pregnant then clearly a very serious offense has been committed.
>   The baby is the evidence.
>   Unless police start to do something, boys will not be frightened off. They will go on getting off scot-free. (ibid.: 4)

Reproductive sexuality, it seems, has been and continues to be focused on women and the figure of the mother. But boys and men are not completely out of the picture. They are 'positioned' through discourse on sexuality and particularly where the 'evidence' of sexual activity is a baby. However, they are 'positioned' in different ways.

Problem fathers – men and reproductive sex/uality

Mostly, men/fathers figure as different sorts of absences. What is the significance of fatherhood for male sex/uality (see Chapter 6)? How is masculine sexuality expressed in reproduction? How are men positioned in discourses constructing reproductive sex/uality?

As far as new reproductive technologies (NRTs) are concerned, men have not figured prominently. Old and new reproductive technologies have focused mainly on 'female infertility'. The most 'high tech' of NRTs have focused on making up for deficits in the female body. However, men are implicated in the causes of female infertility through infection by sexually transmitted diseases (STDs).

The technologies applied to women's bodies are expensive, experimental, cutting edge, glamorous. Historically, male infertility has not often been the object of investigation and treatment, and where it has it has mostly been subject to a low tech, inexpensive 'solution' – donor insemination. This may in turn produce problems for the 'identities' of 'father' and 'child' within the terms of prevailing discourses on the family and familial relations (insinuated by biological/genetic discourse). The male body appears on the periphery of investigations into and treatments of infertility. More recently, male bodies and infertility have become objects of research and new techniques like micro injection of sperm into ova have been used to facilitate conception where male partners have very low sperm counts.[3]

In the deployment of NRTs to help the heterosexual couple have a baby, men's desire has a curious private/public aspect. Men are part of the reproductive process, but in a solitary and peripheral way. The would-be father (possibly sitting in a cubicle with a pile of *Playboy* magazines) is required to masturbate to the point of ejaculation, collect (in the vessel supplied) and hand over his bodily fluids to a health professional. The visible evidence of his solitary sex act is available to a more public view. Men have described feeling alienated during this process and while watching their female partner undergoing the painful procedures involved in NRTs. Men figure as half of the couple longing for a child in discourse which constructs parenthood in terms of blood ties, meaning genetic links to a child. They figure much more prominently when ova are donated and they are the only genetic parent and when surrogacy is the chosen option. Gender relations in reproduction are also transformed in surrogacy where the ova are those of the female partner in the couple.

The supply of sperm, not as a result of heterosexual intercourse, is nonetheless a sex act which affirms a specific aspect of masculine (hetero)sexuality. The expectation is (in NRTs and surrogacy) that this biological function will give rise to the social role of father and the rehabilitation of the infertile couple as the reproductive heterosexual family. When men perform this sex act and hand over their ejaculate to lesbians, it does not follow that they will parent (often, they do not). This possible absence signals a discontinuity between the (male) biological body and ascribed (masculine) gender roles which is as old as the hills and which is currently being targeted by an economic discourse again concerned with the cost to the state of bringing up fatherless families. The man who has fathered children and is not financially supporting them is increasingly constituted as an object of public interest and concern.

The lesbians (discussed earlier) who have revealed the circumstances of their pregnancies – self-insemination using sperm from a donor known to them – are being pressurised to name the father by the Child Support Agency (CSA) or face losing benefits.[4] Had they received donor insemination in a clinical setting, the donor's identity would have been anonymous and protected by law. Since he is known to the women, he is required to pay for the children. The CSA (which has a public image of inefficiency in tracing fathers and making them pay, and setting an appropriate level of payment), articulates a moral discourse which seeks to make men responsible for children and to reinforce the idea that men are fathers, families cannot exist without them, and women and children are dependent on them. Again, this is the product of intersecting moral and economic discourses which construct the heterosexual nuclear family as the core unit in the privatised provision of welfare.

Boys and men are figured as the absent parties in teenage pregnancy and single motherhood. All parties – women who bear children outside of the heterosexual married unit and the men who 'make' them pregnant – are open to the accusation of irresponsibility. The consequences, however, for girls/women and boys/men are different. Accusations of irresponsibility work within existing discourses on gender to position women as having let it (pregnancy) happen, thereby invalidating pregnancy as a decision and deliberate action and positioning (especially poor) women as dependent on men. Men and boys, on the other hand, who enact sex/ualities irresponsibly are represented as driven by overwhelming (almost 'animal') urges and failing to exercise sufficient control over these. They are positioned as dominant and pressurising. This is part of a discourse constituting uneven relations of gender and sexuality which may foreclose other images of masculine sexuality.

In a series of stories about teenage boys becoming fathers, the *Sun* takes an apparently hostile view, asserting that the children born and their mothers will depend on state benefits and so burden the taxpayer with the costs:

> **LUST GENERATION**: This is Robert Tinsley. He is just 17. Soon he will be the father of THREE children by two different girls. They're all living off the State. He thinks he's very clever. . . .
>
> . . . unrepentant Tinsley, who has never worked, thinks he is CLEVER to let the State fork out for his carelessness. (20 May 1997: 4)

The parents of the two girls, MPs and moral campaigners, 'branded the scrounging dad a disgrace'.

The *Sun* explains that Robert Tinsley and his two 16-year-old lovers (who are both pregnant) are all jobless and 'get benefits totalling over £250 per week. Both girls have been found furnished homes'. Robert, apparently, has left his first girlfriend, with whom he has a 16-month-old daughter and who is pregnant with his second child, to live with his new girlfriend who is also pregnant. What does fatherhood involve for him? Both girls say they hardly ever see Robert and have become good friends: 'All he wants is sex and he doesn't care who he hurts. . . . It wouldn't suprise me if he hasn't got another girlfriend on the go already' (ibid.: 5).

The *Sun* appears to articulate a moral discourse by calling him 'shameless', 'unrepentant', 'careless' and a 'love-rat'. Not only has he been reckless, but he does not seem to perceive the error of his ways or care about them. He says he has done nothing wrong and 'wouldn't mind having more children':

> Shameless Tinsley said: 'I love children and am as proud as punch.
> At least I can enjoy watching them grow up while I am young'.

Robert is little more than a child himself but 'that is no excuse for the total lack of self-control that is ruining so many lives'. We should all feel guilty for creating 'an easy-go society in which making girls pregnant is greeted by a shrug of the shoulders' (*Sun*, 20 May 1997: 4). An ambiguity is apparent. Robert is positioned as having a large sexual appetite by all those commenting on his conduct. He is constructed as wanting only one thing – sex (as heterosexual copulation). The evidence of his sexual appetite is in the results – pregnancies (three of them). The sexuality constructed is a masculine heterosexual force which Robert is unable to control. Masculine heterosexuality is constructed as dominating and female sexuality as relatively passive – Robert, of course, 'makes them' pregnant.

The terms 'lust generation' and 'love rat' are not necessarily pejorative – they appear to chastise whilst harbouring a faint admiration for, and actively helping to constitute, the masculine sex drive displayed here. His 'errors' mostly consist of not taking on the moral and financial responsibilities of fatherhood.

Talk of Robert's irresponsibility hinges on the fact that he is jobless, as are the mothers, and the state/taxpayers will have to pay – until he can pay (if ever). It shifts the emphasis a little away from unmarried mothers to unmarried fathers and makes them partly responsible for the breakdown of the traditional married heterosexual nuclear family. According to the *Sun*, Robert is making a 'depressing mockery of family life'. The issue at stake is the survival of the family as an economic and social unit, capable of providing welfare, socialisation and moral education for a new generation of citizens. A (Thatcherite) call for a return to an idealised past of 'traditional Christian (Victorian) moral values' and the regulatory device of 'stigmatisation' is articulated.

> *A generation ago, teenage pregnancy carried a stigma. Your irresponsibility shamed you and your family.* . . . Today, having a baby can be a passport to a council flat and a fortnightly giro. (*Sun*, 20 May 1997: 4)

The vilification of Robert, and other boys like him, is reminiscent of the nineteenth century and fears that the 'unfit' (the poor, unhealthy and under-educated) might be multiplying faster than the better-educated classes who were able to support themselves (Gordon, 1977; Weeks, 1989). The multiplication of 'the unfit' was perceived as undermining the quality of the population. Again, the poor are positioned as undisciplined and uneducated, closer to nature and to animals, and less able to control their desires than educated individuals. Work is seen as a means to distraction and a way of disciplining these unruly bodies. It could also provide for the welfare of any ensuing children.

> The former health minister Sir Gerard Vaughan said: this young man would do far better getting off his backside and finding some work. Then he can help support the children rather than seeking sexual excitement while he has nothing else to do. (*Sun*, 20 May 1997: 5)

Reflecting on the nature of the issues raised by this set of pregnancies, the *Sun*'s agony aunt argues that more sex education is needed to show teenagers like this what having a baby means and about contraception. Again the view is expressed that reproductive sexuality is a route to adulthood for the under-educated young who do not expect to find jobs. Girls are having babies because they think it gives them a job, and boys think it gives them status. The solution is to 'find a path for young people who aren't college material' (ibid.).

Again it is argued that the parents of the teenagers are implicated – as part of a discourse reinforcing the nuclear family as the place of welfare and moral education. The girls' parents, it is stated, should take responsibility for girls' ignorance or gung-ho attitude to their fertility. And 'What about Robert's folks? Has his dad helped him to grow into a responsible young man? I wonder' (ibid.)

In a similar story (28 April 1997: 4–5) the *Sun* tells of

DIRTY DARRON'S 3 KIDS BY 3 GIRLS IN 8 MONTHS

The article states that three women were walking around pregnant with Darron's babies at the same time. Thirty-one-year-old Darron is living with his new lover, leaving two single parent families (his wife with three children, his former girlfriend with one). Again, the taxpayers will collect the bill. The two single parent families cost the taxpayer £300 a week. Darron is being pursued by the Child Support Agency (who have not yet caught him). Details of benefits received by the women are printed. Darron himself was a 'barrow boy', but is also now unemployed.

Referring to Darron as the 'bonking barrow boy', the newspaper assigns him a status similar to Robert's – one of sexual appetite, which is also too big for his age and class. Again, masculine hetero-sex/uality is constructed as a force which is hard to control – and, in this case, is uncontrolled.

On 14 April 1997 the *Sun* printed an article about Britain's youngest grandfather, Dale Wright, aged 29. He was 14 when his own son was born, who has now fathered a daughter at 14. Dale describes being shocked at the birth and says he wished it had not happened. He and his then girl-friend struggled (they split up at 16 and went their separate ways) with being parents at 14 and they could not have managed without the help of their parents. Now, he says, they must give Stephen and his girlfriend the same sort of help. Stephen's mother emphasises that they are not going to claim benefits but will look after themselves, with Stephen's girlfriend and her parents. These statements again reproduce the idea of the family as a self-sufficient system of private welfare.

The proud grandfather is later quoted as saying:

Like father like son . . .
   I couldn't shout at Stephen too much because I'd done exactly the same when I was his age. . . .
   I can't believe I'm really a grandad. . . .
   And it's also incredible that I've got to wait another four years before he can buy me a drink to wet the baby's head. He's certainly a chip off the old block!
(*Sun*, 20 May 1997: 5)

Dale is proud. He seems to be saying that his granddaughter is further con-firmation of his own sexual prowess, expressed through premature reproduction. His sexual appetite has been passed on to his son – the baby is the proof of his vigorous biologically propelled heterosex/uality.

Stephen says he wants to be a good father to his daughter and helps out where he can – feeding her and changing nappies. He says: 'I didn't want this to happen but it did, and now we have got to do the best we can' (ibid.).

A discourse on the responsibilities of nuclear heterosexual families and fathers within them is expressed through the questions directly posed in the text: 'how much of a dad' has Dale been to Stephen? How much is Stephen, despite being happy to be a dad, going to take on the brunt of caring for a baby's needs?

These stories are about youth, class and income. Young jobless men are publically exposed as irresponsible, lacking in self-control, selfish, lustful in generating single families dependent on the state. In contrast, in 1997 the media discussed the 'unconventional' private family arrangements of very rich men (Sir Matthew Harding and Sir James Goldsmith, both of whom have since died). Following their deaths, there have been public disclo-sures about the inheritance of their considerable respective fortunes. It has been revealed that both men had a wife and a mistress, spent time with each and had children with each. Matthew Harding had one wife, with four children, and one mistress, with one child. He spent the week days with his mistress and the weekends with his wife and their children. James Goldsmith, the wealthier of the two men, had several wives and mistresses in succession and eight children by three wives. Public attention has been focused on the distribution of the estates among the surviving 'families', not on the irresponsibilities of their sexual appetites and reproductive prowess. No one asks (publically, at least) how much of a dad was each of them?

These 'stories' both moralise about and naturalise masculine heterosex-uality and its expression in reproduction. Prevailing discourses interpellate women as mothers and men as fathers and position them within a hetero-sexual married family unit. They also produce the idea a child's right to be born into a specific sort of family – to have two parents, one of either gender, who are financially secure and independent. In this way, limits appear to be placed on the extent to which sex, gender and sexuality can be disaggregated in postmodernity. The 'queer' family is marginalised as a grotesque aberration. But this should not foreclose the possibility that, out of the public gaze, subversive plays on gender are enacted. To what extent do ('ordinary') women, and men, recognise themselves in the gendered fig-ures of parenthood thereby constructed? Do subjects variously positioned as women and men want to be addressed in this way?

The discourses articulated through the media texts discussed in this chapter help to produce 'the sexual' as a contested site. One of the conse-quences of viewing sex as 'a performatively enacted signification', rather than a way of being, is that it occasions 'the parodic proliferation and sub-versive play of gendered meanings' (Butler, 1990a: 33). 'Queer families' might be seen as constituting instances of 'the subversive play of gendered meanings', while at the same time being created within heterosexualising, marginalising and disavowing discourses.

'Queer families', entailing a reconfiguration of the family unit and sub-ject positions of mother and father, are constituted and problematised within various discourses which appear to be engaged in reinvigorating the traditional married heterosexual family unit. The enthusiasm directed at the latter activity could be read as symptomatic of the fragility and non-necessity of heterosexuality and the gender identities it prescribes. It indicates that identification, analysis and judgement of 'sexual deviants', along with other marginalised subjects, may fulfil an important normalis-ing function in contemporary society. I explore this idea further in the next chapter, which examines the representation of lesbians in popular culture, on prime time TV.

Notes

1. 'Peter Lilley, the Secretary of State for Social Security, at the Conservative Party Conference in 1992, included "young girls who get pregnant to jump the housing queue" on his "little list of undesirable social phenomena". In 1993, Lilley made a speech at the House of Commons linking the enormity of the costs of state benefits to the demands made by single mothers' (Woodward, 1997: 259).

2. Whilst the 1993 Education Act allowed sex education to be compulsory in maintained secondary schools, amendments to the National Curriculum deleted all references to STDs, HIV/AIDs and sexual behaviour and gave parents the right to withdraw children from sex education in addition to that contained in the National Curriculum. Adler argues that parents should be involved and informed but that pupils have rights to education about sex and personal relationships and, unless it is part of the National Curriculum, not all pupils will receive it (Adler, 1997: 6).

He also suggests that there is a need for a good service for people with STDs; and provision of continuing programmes for particular groups like young homosexu-als and certain ethnic minorities (ibid.: 7).

3. The micro-manipulation of sperm and egg involves removal of ova collected from a woman's body and immature sperm from a man's testicles. Holes are drilled or chemically burned in the egg's outer coating so that sperm can be inserted, or, alternatively, a single sperm might be injected into the egg.

4. The CSA was set up by the last Conservative Government in the UK under the auspices of the Department of Social Security on 5 April 1993.

9

SEXUAL PARODY – LESBIANS IN POPULAR CULTURE[1]

Imitating sex/gender

Genders are neither true nor false, according to Judith Butler, but are produced as 'the truth effects of a discourse of primary and stable identity' (Butler, 1990a: 136). Since there is no true gender, gender performances are all parody and imitation. Thus, drag is not the imitation of one gender by the other, because the relation is not one of copy to original, but of copy to copy. Significantly, *in imitating gender, drag implicitly reveals the imitative structure of gender itself – as well as its contingency'* (ibid.: 137). Parody is not by itself subversive. Rather, it is necessary to investigate how parodic repetitions sometimes are effectively disruptive and troubling and, conversely, how they sometimes become 'domesticated and recirculated as instruments of cultural hegemony' (ibid.: 139).

Here I examine a particular example of sexual parody in popular culture to reveal some of the ways in which practices of femininity and masculinity may be compelled and constrained. I use the notion of gender as performance, and imitation, to make a reading of the BBC's dramatisation of *Portrait of a Marriage* – Nigel Nicolson's account of aspects of his parents' marriage, including the affair of his mother (Vita Sackville West) with a particular woman (Violet Keppel). One of the key features of this drama is the elaboration of butch/femme roles and some highly stylised cross-dressing. Drag appears to present a performance of gender in which a dissonance created between sex and gender. I focus on representations of relations between sex, gender and sexuality (which I have so far collectively termed sex/uality) in *Portrait* and examine the extent to which they generate new and subversive gendered meanings.

My reading develops from ideas and themes elaborated in earlier chapters. In particular, the idea that identity is not an essence nor an attribute of the individual but a positioning, a process, a performance which is always incomplete and must be repeatedly reinvented and re-enacted within the context of history, power and discourse (Butler, 1990a; Hall, 1990). Sex/gender can be viewed as constituted through an infinite range of mundane acts – or practices of femininity and masculinity – which must be repeatedly performed within discourses which both compel and constrain. Also central to my reading is the idea that representation does not describe events but produces them. Media texts can be viewed as participating in the discursive production of understandings of the sexed body, which compel both a limitation and an expansion of possible enactments whereby the body is configured as sexed and specific sex/ualities are made possible.

I have argued that the media help to define a public space in which sex is put on view and exposed as something private and intimate. The transgression of public/private space is central to notions of 'the sexual', which in turn support the dichotomous categories public/private, mind/body, reason/emotions, culture/nature, male/female, white/non-white. I have also suggested that the category 'homosexual' is necessary to define a border constituting heterosexuality and to secure its ontological boundaries. Television potentially involves huge audiences in the production of transgression and reinvention of identities (although I am not making any assumptions about whether or how audiences make use of these images). These themes are elaborated in Chapter 4.

I now consider the various performances of hetero/homo sex/uality enacted through the dramatisation of *Portrait of a Marriage*. This constitutes only one of many possible readings. *Portrait* could, alternatively, be examined for the ways in which it reproduces class relations. To a large extent the theatricality of the sex/uality displayed owes a lot to the personal wealth and social privilege of the individuals involved.

BBC TV's *Portrait of a Marriage* was lavishly produced in the popular genre of historical costume drama and transmitted in prime viewing time. Well before it went on air, journalists' temperatures were soaring. Evidently, explicit lesbianism on the BBC could not be ignored, nor could it be allowed to hog the limelight. Most journalists responded by downplaying the significance of lesbianism and some stressed that the drama told the story of someone torn between two lovers, never mind their sexes. Nigel Nicolson complained to *The Times* that the dramatisation of his book had concentrated on a brief and crazy escapade in the long and otherwise harmonious marriage of his parents, in which love had triumphed over infatuation (Merck, 1993).

Clearly, *Portrait of a Marriage* was already guaranteed success. It was deeply dangerous, but ultimately safe. Lesbianism threatened family life but was brought to heel by an assertion of duty and responsibility and an insistence on the rightful expression of these values through the institution of marriage. Although historically and culturally remote for many viewers, the marriage portrayed in upheaval could not fail to resonate with contemporary questions voiced in media and political discourses about the meaning of marriage to Britain's diverse populations. Evidently, there is increasing concern that marriage may no longer function as a core unit in the social organisation, cohesion and regulation of British society.[2] In this light, *Portrait of a Marriage* appears to put forward prototype terms and conditions for successful heterosexual marriage, with an emphasis on the mutual respect, indulgence and flexibility (within clearly defined limits) of both partners. However, the dramatisation of Vita and Violet's love-making, which was passionate and convincing, cannot be explained away in full by the fragility of early and late twentieth-century marriage. The sex scenes deserve more attention, because, in my view, they also attempt to spell out what it means to *be a sex* and present a precise differentiation of masculinity and femininity.

Sex and the drama of difference

The possibility that *Portrait of a Marriage* may be more about heterosexuality than about homosexuality has been raised by Elizabeth Wilson (1990) and Mandy Merck (1993). Both authors conclude that the drama provides a way of scrutinising heterosexuality and the frailty of modern marriage, which is brought into focus through perversity. Wilson asks whether 'gay love' may be 'the lens through which heterosexual society is desperately peering at its own problematic practices?' (1990: 31). According to Wilson, *Portrait* was broadcast in the context of 'intense cultural ambivalence' as suggested by the 'higher visibility' of homosexuality in the British media at a time of anti-homosexual repression (hot on the heels of Clause 28). Merck adds to this the possibility that the institution of marriage is strengthened by 'the very homosexuality which threatens to destroy it' and by the invention of a 'new man' and 'new woman' (Merck, 1993: 116). However, Merck's analysis needs to be developed to show in detail how particular representations of lesbian sex(uality) contribute to the redefinition of sexual difference and, through this, to the reinforcement of heterosexual relations.

Portrait of a Marriage probably did say a lot less about lesbians than about heterosexuals. However, in my view, the drama's representation of 'gay love' was not transparent, as the metaphor of a lens might suggest; instead lesbian sex was brought into focus and made visible – constituted – through exactly the same discourse as that which was capable of articulating a crisis in heterosexual marital relations. In *Portrait,* the versions of lesbian sex presented on screen were not wild cards or disparate moments of sexual diversity but steady and negative counterparts to revered elements of marriage. Thus, the drama persistently distinguished sexual desire from marriage, infatuation from love. Desire figured largely as homosexual and love belonged to heterosexual marriage. Desire was treacherous, infantile and selfish, whereas marriage was loyal and secure, safeguarded by a sense of duty and responsibility to others. Set in the framework of this series of opposites, Vita and Violet's affair provided a stage for the continuing rehearsal of sex, as an act, an identity and a social position. The representations of lesbian sex in *Portrait* enabled a redefinition not only of the boundaries of marriage but also of what it means to be a sex and, more precisely, what it means to be female. I shall now look more closely at *how* particular representations of lesbian sex simultaneously produced different characterisations of 'woman' and how this contributed to the reproduction of heterosexual relations.

The drama persistently lurched between distinctive moments of gender bending using the familiar genre of drag. Each lesbian sex scene was preceded by Vita's theatrical 'crossing over', in which her dress, deportment and conduct were dramatically transformed. More precisely, they and she were *masculinised*. When Vita suddenly appeared in jodhpurs both Harold and Violet commented independently that she looked both mannish and fetching. Their communications of sexual approval appeared to be flavoured by their viewing of Vita as less feminine and, because of it, a potential seducer. Harold and Violet's comments implied that she had become more obviously sexual because she had become more masculine. Given Harold and Violet's already declared interests in same sex sex, the brief exchanges around the jodhpurs contributed to a heightened sense of muddled sexuality and discontinuity between sex and gender. Viewers may have felt compelled to wonder whether Harold desired Vita as a woman or a quasi-man. Violet, who had always desired Vita, could openly express it now that Vita was less like a woman and more like a man. It was Vita's unfeminine conduct which Violet found especially appealing. Thus, Vita's masculinisation crudely signalled a newly discovered perversity. Now, more than before, Vita was capable of having sex with Violet. Viewers were led to believe that her desire for Violet was framed through masculine eyes.

Through this example of drag the active pursuit of desire and its fulfilment in sex was made entirely the prerogative of masculinity, and lesbianism became visible only through these particular enactments of butch/femme stereotypes. This version of lesbianism, and the narrowly defined version of femininity it implied, was crassly accentuated in a series of very camp scenes. As a prelude to sex, Vita was seen running across fields and leaping over gates in an athletic, uninhibited way while Violet, dressed much less practically, stumbled and flapped helplessly behind, waiting for a display of gallantry by Vita. Similarly, in anticipation of scenes in which the two women were seen naked in bed, Vita appeared in drag as Violet's working-class soldier husband when the couple contrived to spend a night together in a bed and breakfast and as her flamboyant and dashing tango partner in a bar during their first trip to France.

Drag in *Portrait* was significant because it made sure that lesbianism would be interpreted as a replication of heterosexual relations and that desire would be seen as inevitably heterosexual in its expression. Moreover, heterosexuality was rendered identical with an expression of desire from the position of a masculine subject. The heterosexualisation of Vita and Violet's affair reached its conclusion as Vita competed with Denys Trefusis for sexual rights to Violet. Vita insisted that Violet was sexually faithful to her despite marrying Denys. The drama pursued this insistence to the point of explicit violence when, on hearing that Violet had slept with her husband, Vita raped her. In this way, lesbianism was brought into focus and made visible through an emphasis on (hetero)sexual fidelity and property, and the defence of these through violence. This is not to say that violence between lesbians does not and cannot exist. However, Vita and Violet's conduct was most readily understood from a particular heterosexual point of view. This was underlined by a focus on kissing and cuddling, at one extreme, and rape, at the other, rather than the different and more obvious ways in which women may find pleasure in sex. In many scenes, passionate kissing petered out to leave a space usually filled by images of heterosexual copulation. Viewers were directed towards thinking of heterosexual penetration or drawing a blank – what do lesbians *do* in bed? The outcome was likely to be another representation of heterosexuality as the proper expression of desire. Nothing about *Portrait* contradicted this. The net effect was that Vita and Violet appeared to be copying heterosexuals.

A heterosexual economy of sexuality relies upon the idea that sex is a dichotomous and exclusive category, which forms the basis of gender as a discrete identity and social position. The logic of heterosexuality assumes that male is directly connected to masculine and to man, and female to feminine and woman (Butler, 1990a). This sequence of association supports the expression of desire in heterosexual reproduction. *Portrait of a Marriage* was very good at sticking to and reinforcing the pairs of opposites – male/female, masculine/feminine, man/woman – which are necessary to the reproduction of heterosexuality. The drama ensured that the connections between male and man, and female and woman, were incontrovertible. The sex of the characters was never in dispute, nor was their social position as man or woman. In addition, 'sex' appeared immutable and fixed because 'gender' seemed more plastic and variable (Butler, 1990a). Manifestations of homosexuality could be explained as 'getting into' or 'putting on' the gender contra-indicated by one's sex. Since homosexuality was represented as self-evidently abnormal, the imputed chain of causality linking sex with heterosexual reproduction is further reinforced. If gender was successfully represented as flexible and malleable, it was also thereby rendered more amenable to remedy and regulation, in this case by the (re)assumption of womanly duties. Thus, between sex scenes, Vita was seen tucking her children up in bed and at dinner with Harold and his parents and Violet was seen walking down the aisle with Denys.

The probable connections and possible disconnections between sex and gender were openly verbalised in a scene in which Harold confided in his friend, Reggie, that he was made miserable by Vita's passion for Violet and was himself 'no ladies' man'. Reggie replies that Vita was very much 'what they call a man's woman'. As he explained, this meant 'a woman who's tough and honourable. Female rather than feminine'. Since it is possible to be female, whilst being either feminine or un-feminine, Reggie also implied that femininity was more pliable than sex. His statements further reinforced the idea that masculinity was the proper effect of a male body and femininity the effect of a female body. Variations in the cultural enactment of gender gave rise to a 'man's woman' in contrast to any other sort of woman. Femaleness appeared fixed only because it was assumed to be equal to a pre-given unequivocal anatomical morphology.

The immutability of sex is apparently written on the female body. Hence it was highly significant that viewers were made so aware of Vita's crossing over and that her masculinisation was intermittent. It was important too that Vita was shown unambiguously to possess a female anatomy. This was emphasised throughout the drama in which she was filmed in various states of undress. Scenes showing her naked in bed or sitting around in her underwear, appeared to expose and highlight the essentially female contours of her body. In the first episodes, the logical and fruitful expression of her anatomical sex in heterosexual reproduction is represented in scenes showing her as Harold's wife and Ben and Nigel's mother. When not in drag, Vita appears in 'the most fetishistic female costumes of the drama', wearing glittering dresses, jewel-studded hairpieces, extravagant furs and hats (Merck, 1993: 115). The act of crossing over reveals that masculinity and femininity consist of a particular series of investments in a sexed body, which is always already accepted as irrefutably male or female. The fact that lesbian sex becomes possible when an obviously female body is uncharacteristically presented in masculine attire, implies that lesbianism arises from an irregularity or disjunction in relations between sex as anatomy (body), sense of self (identity) and social category (woman).

Sexual discontinuities were partly echoed in the characterisation of Harold as gentle, indulgent and gay. His character was, to some extent, demasculinised. However, he didn't have to get into a frock. He maintained an air of paternalism throughout the drama. When pushed too far, he put his foot down, asserted his authority and prevented Vita from meeting Violet in France. His homosexuality was represented as much less a problem than Vita's passion for Violet.

Harold's deviant sexuality was phrased in terms of confession and absolution, disease and treatment, with the implication that it was manageable by words or drugs. Initially, his penchant for sex with men was revealed through his confession that he was being treated for syphilis. Later, in conversation with Reggie, Harold explained that his homosexuality was functional, like shitting and eating, but did not provide a motive for life as did marriage to Vita. Reggie pointed out that sex between men was also therefore as essential as those other functions, a matter of (carefully organised) necessity. In contrast, sex between women was a voracious appetite potentially raging out of control. Gayness appeared to complement heterosexual marital relations, whereas lesbianism threatened to destroy them. Importantly, Harold's insistence that Vita, as his wife and the mother of his children, was central in his life reaffirmed the causal logic linking sex (maleness and femaleness) with the expression of sexuality through procreation within marriage. The fact that he was side-tracked by sex with men was less significant than achieving and maintaining this all-important familial status. Heterosexual family life filled the chasm opened by Harold's announcement of his sexually acquired disease whereupon sexuality in marriage appeared to fizzle out. Harold's conversation with Reggie and Vita and Violet's repeated assertions that infidelities, especially those of the perverse kind, didn't matter and could be better pursued within marriage served further to subordinate deviant sexuality to heterosexual marriage. These statements emphasised the basic important characteristics of a successful and enduring marriage, in this context love born out of a sense of duty, subscription to the same (ruling-class) values and companionship.

The apparent distinction drawn between same sex sex involving men and that involving women is significant because it both defines the limits and limitations of perversity and, importantly, says something more about women. It suggests that women are in possession of a sexuality which is wild and boundless and that women themselves are completely without (self) restraint. The potential havoc caused by untempered female sexuality is compounded when women get together for sex. The possibility of deliverance from this (fantasy of) female destructiveness is signalled through the interruption and curtailment of lesbianism by the arrival of a masculine subject, in this case, the bridegroom Denys helped into the role by Harold.

Portrait of a Marriage offers two assurances: that maleness and femaleness are basically distinct and enduring; and that masculinity and femininity are more pliant and prone to deviation but also amenable to remedy and renegotiation. Thus, lesbianism signals the limitations of gender roles within marriage and opens up the possibility of redefining and restabilising the borders of marriage, masculinity and femininity.

Surely, *Portrait of a Marriage* must be applauded for making lesbians more visible and producing a greater popular cultural awareness and acceptability of lesbianism and *difference*? It did at least transgress the usual boundaries of sexuality as represented in standard television dramas. Indeed, although lesbianism was made visible through the lens of heterosexuality, the drama was also open to different readings. Lesbians watching *Portrait*, whether they considered the lingering passionate kisses and gentle (non-genital) stroking in the afterglow of having 'done it' erotic or insipid, could variously 'read in' their own fantasies and predilections. Furthermore, an exploration of possible 'lesbian' readings would reveal that women having sex with women, however they dress and whatever they do, is not the same as, nor simply a copy of, heterosexual sex. If Vita and Violet's sex seemed like a copy rather than the real thing, it was because desire between the two women was effectively framed from a particular heterosexual point of view. This is not to say that the rape was any less violent or abhorrent, nor that the images of lesbians were any less negative than I have already suggested. This line of argument inevitably generates other concerns.

The idea that there is a real or genuine heterosexuality, or masculinity/

femininity, to be impersonated can be challenged in terms of Judith Butler's arguments that gender is performance and that all gender performances are imitation and parody. All performances of gender and heterosexuality are copies, since there is no true gender.

Just because BBC producers judge that mass audiences can stomach tastefully filmed sexual deviations does not of course mean that these audiences accept them. There is always the possibility that such productions will provoke antagonism towards, or encourage exploitation of, those who are represented as different. The other major difficulty, for BBC producers and lesbian critics alike, lies in a tendency to characterise homo- and heterosexual and sub- and mainstream culture(s) as direct opposites, thereby also implying that each is a coherent and distinctive whole. Again, this places limits on sexual diversity by implying that dykes are basically the same and so are straights.

In an article entitled '"Doing it": representations of lesbian sex' Kitzinger and Kitzinger (1993) argue that the costs of media representations of lesbian sex hugely outweigh the benefits. They suggest that the invisibility of lesbians and lesbian sex may be preferable to the alternatives which invariably represent women who have sex with women as 'predatory, crazed, psychopathic sadists' and lesbian sexuality as 'dangerous and perverted, inextricably intertwined with violence and despair' (Kitzinger and Kitzinger, 1993: 10). In addition, representations of lesbian sex are widespread in heterosexual male pornography and often represented as 'foreplay' or warming up for men: 'lesbianism rarely withstands the arrival of the male on the scene' (ibid.: 11). If a man does not intervene, lesbian sex is a poor substitute, leaving an unfulfilled sexuality and inviting the jibe that all a lesbian needs is a good fuck (by a man). Kitzinger and Kitzinger also point out that, as well as being portrayed through a male gaze, lesbians are often assigned a male point of view. The suggestion that lesbians too can enjoy films produced for heterosexual male consumption necessitates them viewing other women through a male gaze and objectifying them. Kitzinger and Kitzinger reject the idea that lesbians can appropriate these images and remake them for their own pleasure and that this in itself constitutes a radical transformation. They argue that the appropriation of symbols of domination by lesbians reinforces rather than transgresses heterosexual customs and violences. They discuss the production of representations of lesbian sex by lesbians for lesbians and express concern that all 'lesbian-generated images' are also vulnerable to male appropriation and pornographic interpretations. One possible solution, they suggest, 'is simply to refuse to collaborate with the production or distribution of lesbian sex scenes' (Kitzinger and Kitzinger, 1993: 16–17). They ask:

> If we construct lesbian representations of lesbian sex, how do we know that we have done so *as lesbians*, and from 'a lesbian gaze', as opposed to adopting a male gaze and utilising the conventions of male pornography? Simply claiming that they are 'by women for women' doesn't solve the problem. (ibid.: 20)

Kitzinger and Kitzinger reflect on whether lesbians should settle for positive portrayals of female friendships, for example supportive, intimate
and warm relationships between women in the films *Thelma and Louise*,
Bagdad Café and *Salmonberries*. Just because lesbian sex has been repressed,
they argue, it doesn't mean that now it has to be expressed.

I have several problems with Kitzinger and Kitzinger's argument.
Mainly, I am worried by the ideas that *a* distinctively *lesbian* gaze exists,
albeit open to contamination by a male gaze, and that *lesbian* representations are possible, albeit vulnerable to being ripped off by men. Firstly,
these ideas tend to 'essentialise' the categories 'lesbians' and 'men' – that is,
reproduce them as the fixed ground from which subjects act, rather than,
as Butler (1990a) argues, as produced through the very acts said to be their
effects. Secondly, the idea of a lesbian gaze as opposed to a male gaze
tends to reproduce the categories 'lesbians', 'lesbian sex' and 'men' as singular and coherent entities and positionings. This, in turn, precludes the
articulation of further possible sexual diversities and the complexity of
the (power) relations through which they become visible to differently situated viewers. This tendency is reinforced by a discussion of authenticity,
motivation and interpretation. Thus, the Kitzingers question whether particular lesbian characters are accurate or distorted representations of
lesbians. They want to know which intentions lie behind a particular portrait of lesbianism and how it flavours public perceptions of lesbians. As a
consequence, their analysis generates an investment in the idea that a
common and general deviant 'experience' exists and is capable of representation and offers a singular viewing position for productions like
Portrait of a Marriage which is *de facto* lesbian. This style of analysis ends up
discriminating and defending a true sexuality from a false one and, in the
process, represents lesbianism narrowly as opposite and 'other' for a seamless version of heterosexuality. It assumes that the media reflect and
describe – either accurately or inaccurately – authentic identity. It also
invests in the idea that reality can be distinguished from fantasy and fact
from fiction rather than inquiring as to how some cultural configurations
come to occupy the privileged place of 'the real' (Butler, 1990a). Further, by
implying that meanings which attach to cultural forms are fixed, for example a masculine gaze or male appropriation, the possibilities for effecting
political shifts to enable new representations are so severely curtailed as to
be impossible. A masculine gaze, used in this way, presupposes and reinforces the same discrete dichotomous versions of sex and gender necessary
to the perpetuation of heterosexual relations.

Portrait demonstrates some of the ways in which performances of
gender are repeatedly brought into focus through and made to reproduce
'its binary frame' (Butler, 1990a: 140) – for example through references to a
naturalised maternal body, inhabited by Vita when not in drag. It articulates a discourse on the nature of masculinity and femininity and the place
of sex in heterosexual marriage.

In my view, an analysis of the representation of lesbians in popular culture must resist assigning a univocal position to a lesbian audience. This goes equally for the representation of any other category of persons. The use of 'we' and 'lesbian' as self-evident and cohesive terms is based on the assumption that they simultaneously refer to an individual sense of self or identity and a collective social position. The political allure of identity and the collective action it makes possible may sometimes foreclose an articulation of diverse other political subject positions (Butler, 1990b). Not all women who have sex with other women call themselves lesbians and, if they do, are not lesbians in the same way. Lesbian may be one of the many identities to which an individual lays claim, and not necessarily the first or most frequent. Being old, black or unemployed may be a more obvious reference point for some. The BBC representation of Vita and Violet's sexual attraction to each other is a case in point, demonstrating that having sex, however passionately and wholeheartedly, does not necessarily lead to the assumption of an individual or collective lesbian identity. Indeed, the drama showed forcefully that lesbian sex did not provide sufficient grounds for a shared world view. Marriage, on the other hand, embodied a solid and reliable stock of common values. For this reason, the object of analysis in reviewing *Portrait of a Marriage* must be a peculiar, and singular, version of lesbian sex and *not* lesbian(s) as an identity or social group.

I argued earlier that the dramatisation of *Portrait of a Marriage* articulated a separation of sex and gender, and in the process created a version of homosexuality which was useful in shoring up heterosexual marital relations. The drama reinforced the idea that biological sex is fixed and gives rise to gender as an intepretation of this. However, as I have already argued, sex is equally inconsistent and also constructed in history and discourse. Sex must be repeatedly produced/enacted. In the unfolding drama of *Portrait,* representations of (naked) female bodies can be read as attempts to reconstitute corporeal boundaries for sex and an anchor for women as a generic entity. Woman and lesbian must be seen as inconsistent and in need of being repeatedly invented. Refusing a view of perversity as a steady and reliable counterpart of various elements of heterosexuality must be the necessary corollary of refusing a globalising concept of woman.

Representations of lesbian sex, whoever produces them, imply particular characterisations of lesbians and women which are qualified and conditional, setting limits to and regulating their possible meanings. The images of lesbian sex scattered throughout *Portrait of a Marriage* are deeply embedded in a specific cultural and historical context. They are bound to resonate differently for women who have sex with women in the 1990s according to the material and political conditions of their lives and the diverse political subject positions they may occupy on the basis of race, class and sexuality. In this way, the political importance of discussing images of lesbian sex in *Portrait* and drawing out their possible meanings, to different viewers in different contexts, is that it enables an articulation of different previously excluded subject positions and aspects of perversity. Through discussion of its omissions and limitations, *Portrait of a Marriage* enables an articulation of more elements of sexual diversity and makes it possible to resist the deployment of 'homosexual' as the negative counterpart to, and element in the regulation of, heterosexual relations.

Notes

1. Sections of this chapter appeared in Harding, J. (1994) 'Making a drama out of difference.'

2. As Mandy Merck (1993: 114) points out, the autumn 1990 transmission of *Portrait of a Marriage* coincided roughly with railing against increases in divorce and single motherhood at the Conservative Party Conference. At the 1993 Conservative Party Conference, single motherhood was again in part blamed for social disintegration and lawlessness.

REFERENCES

Adler, M. (1997) 'An act of betrayal', *Guardian*, 30 July: Society section.

Alexander, S. (1976) 'Women's work in nineteenth century London', in Mitchell, J. and Oakley, A. (eds). *The Rights and Wrongs of Women*. Harmondsworth, Middlesex: Penguin.

Allen, R. (1996a) 'The last generation', *The Times Higher Education Supplement*, 10 May.

Allen, R. (1996b) 'Plastic peril', *The Times Higher Education Supplement*, 7 June.

Barsky, A. (1988) 'The paradox of health', *The New England Journal of Medicine*, 318, 7: 114–18.

Birke, L. and Vines, G. (1987) 'Beyond nature versus nurture: process and biology in the development of gender', *Women's Studies International Forum*, 10, 6: 114–18.

Blier, R. (1984) *Science and Gender: A Critique of Biology and its Theories on Women*. New York: Pergamon Press.

Briggs, A. and Cobley, P. (1998) *The Media: An Introduction*. Harlow: Longman.

Browne, S. (1915) 'The sexual variety and variability among women and their bearing upon social reconstruction', in Rowbotham 1977a.

Butler, J. (1990a) *Gender Trouble. Feminism and the Subversion of Identity*. New York and London: Routledge.

Butler, J. (1990b) 'Gender trouble, feminist theory, and psychoanalytic discourse', in Nicholson, L. (ed.). *Feminism/Postmodernism*. New York and London: Routledge.

Butler, J. (1991) 'Imitation and gender insubordination', in Fuss 1991.

Butler, J. (1992a) 'Contingent foundations: feminism and the question of "postmodernism"', in Butler and Scott 1992.

Butler, J. (1992b) 'Sexual inversions'. In Stanton 1992.

Butler, J. and Scott, J. (eds) (1992) *Feminists Theorize the Political*. New York and London: Routledge.

Chodorow, N. (1978) *The Reproduction of Mothering: Psychoanalysis and the Sociology of Gender*. Berkeley: University of California Press.

Clarke, A. (1995) 'Modernity, postmodernity and reproductive processes, ca. 1890–1990, or "Mommy, where do cyborgs come from anyway?"' in Hables Gray, C. (ed.). *The Cyborg Handbook*. New York and London: Routledge.

Clifford, J. (1986) 'Partial truths', in Clifford, J. and Marcus, G. (eds). *Writing Culture. The Poetics and Politics of Ethnography*. Berkeley and Los Angeles: University of California Press.

Coney, S. (1991) *The Menopause Industry. A Guide to Medicine's 'Discovery' of the Mid-Life Woman*. Auckland: Penguin Books.

Connor, S. (1995) 'Should we ban the suspects?' Cover story, *Independent*, 26 July.

Cooper, G. (1996) 'Brussels demands names in baby-brands scare', *Independent*, 29 May.

Davidoff, L. and Westover, B. (eds) (1986) *Our Work, Our Lives, Our Worlds*. London: Macmillan.

Deleuze, G. and Guattari, F. (1983) *Anti-Oedipus. Capitalism and Schizophrenia*. Minneapolis: University of Minnesota Press.

Delgardo, M. and Clarke, N. (1996) 'Doctors under siege in baby milk scare', *Evening Standard*, 28 May.

Department of Health (1992) *The Health of the Nation*. London: HMSO.

Dillner, L. (1996) 'Green with envy – doctors at large', *The Guardian*, 7 May.

Dinnerstein, D. (1978) *The Rocking of the Cradle and the Ruling of the World*. London: Souvenir Press.

Diprose, R. and Ferrel, R. (1991) *Cartographies. Poststructuralism and the Mapping of Bodies and Spaces*. Sydney: Allen and Unwin.

Douglas, M. (1990) 'Risk as a forensic resource', *Daedalus*, Fall: 1–16.

Dugdale, A. (1988) 'Keller's degendered science', *Thesis Eleven*, 21: 117–28.

Emsley, J. (1996) 'Science: molecule of the month: new suits for old bottles. Forget the scare stories. Phthalates are cheap, versatile and recyclable', *Independent*, 17 June.

Flax, J. (1990) 'Postmodernism and gender relations in feminist theory', in Nicholson, L. (ed.). *Feminism/Postmodernism*. New York and London: Routledge.

Foucault, M. (1976) *The Birth of the Clinic. An Archaeology of Medical Perception*. London: Tavistock.

Foucault, M. (1979) *Discipline and Punish. The Birth of the Prison*. New York: Vintage Books.

Foucault, M. (1980a) 'The eye of power', in Gordon 1980.

Foucault, M. (1980b) 'Body/Power' in Gordon 1980.

Foucault, M. (1981) *The History of Sexuality. Volume One. An Introduction*. Harmondsworth, Middlesex: Penguin Books.

Foucault, M. (1986) *The Archaeology of Knowledge*. London: Tavistock.

Frank, R. (1922) 'The ovary and the endocrinologist', *Journal of the American Medical Association*, 78, 3: 181–5.

Fuss, D. (ed.) (1991) *Inside/Out. Lesbian Theories, Gay Theories*. London and New York: Routledge.

Gagnon, J. H. and Parker, R. G. (1995) 'Conceiving sexuality', in Parker and Gagnon 1995.

Gagnon, J. H. and Simon, W. (1973) *Sexual Conduct: The Sources of Human Sexuality*. London: Hutchinson.

Gallagher, C. and Laqueur, T. (eds) (1987) *The Making of the Modern Body: Sexuality and Society in the Nineteenth Century*. Los Angeles and London: University of California Press.

Gallop, J. (1988) *Thinking through the Body*. New York: Columbia University Press.

Giddens, A. (1993) *The Transformation of Intimacy. Sexuality, Love and Eroticism in Modern Societies*. Cambridge: Polity Press.

Goldman, L. and Tosteson, A. (1991) 'Uncertainty about postmenopausal estrogen' (Editorial), *New England Journal of Medicine*, 235, 11: 800–2.

Gordon, C. (ed.) (1980) *Power/Knowledge: Selected Interviews and Other Writings. (1972–1977) by Michel Foucault*. New York: Pantheon Books.

Gordon, L. (1977) *Women's Body, Women's Right: A Social History of Birth Control in America*. New York: Penguin Books.

Gorman, T. and Whitehead, M. (1989) *The Amarant Book of Hormone Replacement Therapy*. London: Pan Books.

Grant, L. (1994) 'Fertility rights', *Guardian*, 29 January: 6–9.

Greer, G. (1991) *The Change. Women, Ageing and the Menopause*. London: Hamish Hamilton.

Gross, L. (1989) 'Out of the mainstream', in Seiter, E., Borchers, H., Kreutzner, G. and Warth, E. (eds). *Remote Control*. London: Routledge.

Grosz, E. (1987) 'Towards a corporeal feminism', *Australian Feminist Studies*, 5: 1–16.

Grosz, E. (1990) 'The body of signification', in Fletcher, J. and Benjamin, A. (eds). *Abjection, Melancholia, and Love. The Work of Julia Kristeva*. London and New York: Routledge.

Grosz, E. (1994) *Volatile Bodies: Towards a Corporeal Feminism*. Sydney: Allen and Unwin.

Grosz, E. and Probyn, E. (1995) *Sexy Bodies. The Strange Carnalities of Feminism*. London and New York: Routledge.

Gruner, P. and Revill, J. (1995) 'Infertility due to "gender-bender drugs"', *Evening Standard*, 25 July.

Habermas, J. (1994) 'The emergence of the public sphere'. In Polity, 1994.

Hall, S. (1990) 'Cultural identity and diaspora', in Rutherford 1990b.

Hall, S. (1992) 'The question of cultural identity', in Hall et al. 1992.

Hall, S. (ed.) (1997) *Representation. Cultural Representations and Signifying Practices*. London, Thousand Oaks and New Delhi: Sage Publications/ Open University.

Hall, S., Held, D. and McGrew, T. (eds) (1992) *Modernity and its Futures*. Cambridge: Polity Press.

Hamer, D. and Budge, B. (eds) (1994) *The Good, the Bad and the Gorgeous. Popular Culture's Romance with Lesbianism*. London: Pandora.

Haraway, D. (1989a) 'The biopolitics of postmodern bodies: determinations of self in immune system discourse', *Differences*, 1, 1: 3–43.

Haraway, D. (1989b) *Primate Visions: Gender, Race, and Nature in the World of Modern Science*. New York: Routledge.

Haraway, D. (1991) *Simians, Cyborgs and Women. The Reinvention of Nature*. New York: Routledge.

Harding, J. (ed.) (1986) *Perspectives on Gender and Science*. Basingstoke: Falmer Press.

Harding, J. (1993) 'Regulating sex: constructions of the postmenopausal woman in discourses on hormone replacement therapy'. PhD thesis, University of Technology, Sydney.

Harding, J. (1994) 'Making a drama out of difference: *Portrait of a Marriage*', in Hamer and Budge 1994.

Harding, J. (1996) 'Sex and control: the hormonal body', *Body and Society*, 2, 1: 99–111.

Harding, J. (1997) 'Bodies at risk. Sex, surveillance and hormone replacement therapy', in Petersen, A. and Bunton, R. (eds). *Foucault, Health and Medicine*. London and New York: Routledge.

Harding, S. (1986) *The Science Question in Feminism*. Milton Keynes: Open University Press.

Harding, S. (1990) 'Feminism, science, and the anti-enlightenment critiques', in Nicholson, L. (ed.). *Feminism/Postmodernism*. New York and London: Routledge.

Harding, S. and Hintikka, M. (eds) (1983) *Discovering Reality: Feminist Perspectives on Epistemology, Metaphysics, Methodology and Philosophy of Science*. Boston: Reidel.

Harding, S. and O'Barr, J. (eds) (1987) *Sex and Scientific Inquiry*. Chicago and London: University of Chicago Press.

Harvey, L. (1989) 'The post-modernist turn in feminist philosophy of science', *Arena*, 88: 119–33.

Himmelweit, S. (1988) 'More than "a woman's right to choose"', *Feminist Review*, 29: 38–56.

Hite, S. (1994) *Women as Revolutionary Agents of Change. The Hite Reports: Sexuality, Love and Emotion*. London: Hodder and Stoughton.

Hubbard, R. (1988) 'Science, facts, and feminism', *Hypatia*, 3, 1: 3–17.

Hubbard, R., Henifin, M. and Fried, B. (eds) (1982) *Biological Women : The Convenient Myth*. Bloomington: Indiana University Press.

Human Fertility and Embryology Authority (HFEA) (1993) *Donated Ovarian Tissue in Embryo Research and Assisted Conception. Public Consultation Document*. London: HFEA.

Hunt, L. (1996) 'Breast is best, but not in public', *Independent on Sunday*, 28 July.

Imber, B. and Tuana, N. (1988) 'Feminist perspectives on science', *Hypatia*, 3, 1: 139–44.

Institute for Environment and Health (IEH) (1995) *Environmental Oestrogens: Consequences to Human Health and Wildlife*. Leicester: Institute for Environment and Health.

Irigaray, L. (1985) *The Speculum of the Other Woman*. Ithaca, NY: Cornell University Press.

Irigaray, L.(1988) *This Sex Which Is Not One*. Ithaca, NY: Cornell University Press.

Jacobus, M., Keller, E. and Shuttleworth, S. (eds) (1990) *Body/Politics. Women and the Discourses of Science*. New York and London: Routledge.

Jenkins, J. (1991) *Rethinking History*. London and New York: Routledge.

Jenkins, R. and Nuttall, N. (1996) 'Concern grows over suspect baby milk', *The Times*, 28 May.

Johnstone, A. (1995) 'Rise and fall of male fertility: Anne Johnstone explores the vexing issue of research which suggests foetuses are being feminised by oestrogens in the environment', *The Herald*, 26 July.

Katz, J. N. (1990) 'The invention of heterosexuality', *Socialist Review*, 21, 1 (February): 7–34.

Keller, E. (1983) 'Gender and science', in Harding and Hintikka 1983.

Keller, E. (1985) *Reflections on Gender and Science*. New Haven: Yale University Press.

Keller, E. (1987) 'Feminism and science', in Harding and O'Barr 1987.

Keller, E. and Grontkowski, C. (1983) 'The mind's eye', in Harding and Hintikka 1983.

Kembler, S. (1995) 'Medicine's new vision?' in Lister, M. (ed.). *The Photographic Image in Digital Culture*. London and New York: Routledge.

Kirkup, G. and Smith Keller, L. (eds) (1992) *Inventing Women. Science, Technology and Gender*. Cambridge: Polity Press/ Open University.

Kitzinger, J. and Kitzinger, C. (1993) '"Doing it": representations of lesbian sex', in Griffin, G. (ed.). *Outwrite. Lesbianism and Popular Culture*. London: Pluto Press.

Klein, R. (1992) 'The unethics of hormone replacement therapy', *Bioethics News*, 11, 3: 24–37.

Knorr-Cetina, K. and Mulkay, M. (eds) (1983) *Science Observed. Perspectives on the Social Study of Science*. London: Sage Publications.

Kristeva, J. (1982) *Powers of Horror. An Essay on Abjection*. New York: Columbia University Press.

Kristeva, J. (1986) 'The system and the speaking subject', in Moi 1986.

Kuhn, A. (1984) 'Public versus private: the case of indecency and obscenity', *Leisure Studies*, 3: 55–65.

Laclau, E. and Mouffe, C. (1985) *Hegemony and Socialist Strategy: Towards a Radical Democratic Politics*. London: Verso.

Lambton, C. (1993) 'Science: Mamas maketh man – why has human sperm count declined?' *Guardian*, 11 February.

Lancet, (1991) 'More than hot flushes' (Editorial), 338: 917–18.

Laqueur, T. (1987) 'Orgasm, generation, and the politics of reproductive biology', in Gallagher and Laqueur 1987.

Laqueur, T. (1990) *Making Sex: Body and Gender from the Greeks to Freud*. Cambridge, MA and London: Harvard University Press.

Latour, B. (1983) 'Give me a laboratory and I will raise the world', in Knorr-Cetina and Mulkay 1983.

Latour, B. and Woolgar, S. (1979) *Laboratory Life: The Social Construction of Scientific Facts*. Beverley Hills: Sage Publications.

Law, M., Wald, N. and Meade, T. (1991) 'Strategies for prevention of osteoporosis and hip fracture', *British Medical Journal*, 303: 453–9.

Lawson, N. (1996) 'Parents have a right to all information', *The Times*, 29 May.

Lean, G. (1996) 'Is even baby's milk being poisoned now?', *Daily Mail*, 27 May.

Long Hall, D. (1973) 'Biology, sex hormones and sexism in the 1920s', *The Philosophical Forum*, V, 1–2: 81–96.

Losche, D. (1989/90) 'Frankenstein stalks the Coral Gardens: the cult of secrecy in the Abelam', *Australian Journal of Art*, 8: 6–18.

Losche, D. (1990) 'Transit zone: Toni Warburton', *Art and Australia*, 28, 1: 90–3.

Love, N. (1991) 'Politics and voice(s) : an empowerment/knowledge regime', *Differences: A Journal of Feminist Cultural Studies*, 3,1: 85–103.

Lupton, D. (1995a) *The Imperative of Health. Public Health and the Regulated Body*. London, Thousand Oaks, New Delhi: Sage Publications.

Lupton, D. (1995b) *Medicine as Culture. Illness, Disease and the Body in Western Societies*. London, Thousand Oaks and New Delhi: Sage Publications.

Lupton, D. (1997) 'Foucault and the medicalization critique', in Petersen and Bunton 1997.

Lyon, D. (1994) *The Electronic Eye. The Rise of Surveillance Society*. Cambridge: Polity Press.

McLennan, A. (1991) 'Hormone replacement therapy and the menopause' (Australian Menopause Society Consensus Statement), *Medical Journal of Australia*, 155: 43–4.

McLennan, A. (1992) 'Menopause and preventive medicine' (Editorial), *Australian Family Physician*, 21, 3: 205.

MacLennan, G. (1992) 'The Enlightenment Project revisited', in Hall et al. 1992.

McNair, B. (1996) *Mediated Sex, Pornography and Postmodern Culture*. London, New York, Sydney, Auckland: Arnold.

McQuail, D. (1994) *Mass Communication Theory. An Introduction*. 3rd Edition. London, Thousand Oaks and New Delhi: Sage Publications.

Marks, E. and de Courtivron, I. (eds) (1981) *New French Feminisms. An Anthology*. Brighton: Harvester Wheatsheaf.

Marks, K. and Copley, J. (1996) 'All brands of baby milk may contain chemicals', *Daily Telegraph*, 28 May.

Martin, E. (1989) *The Woman in the Body. A Cultural Analysis of Reproduction*. Milton Keynes: Open University Press.

Martin, E. (1990) 'Science and women's bodies: forms of anthropological knowledge', in Jacobus et al. 1990.

Merck, M. (1993) *Perversions. Deviant Readings*. London: Virago.

Mitchell, J. (1975) *Psychoanalysis and Feminism*. Harmondsworth, Middlesex: Penguin Books.

Mitchell, J. and Rose, J. (eds) (1982) *Feminine Sexuality. Jacques Lacan and the École freudienne*. London: Macmillan Press.

Moi, T. (ed.) (1986) *The Kristeva Reader*. Oxford: Basil Blackwell.

Moon, T. (1991) 'Estrogens and disease prevention' (Editorial), *Archives of Internal Medicine*, 151: 17–18.

Morris, S. (1996) 'We know best, says minister in milk scare', *Daily Mail*, 28 May.

National Women's Health Network (1989) *Taking Hormones and Women's Health: Choices, Risks and Benefits*. Washington: National Women's Health Network.

Nicholson, L. (ed.) (1990) *Feminism/Postmodernism*. New York and London: Routledge.

Oudshoorn, N. (1990) 'On the making of sex hormones: research materials and the production of knowledge', *Social Studies of Science*, 20: 5–33.

Oudshoorn, N. (1994) *Beyond the Natural Body. An Archaeology of Sex Hormones*. London and New York: Routledge.

Parker, R. G. and Gagnon, J. H. (eds) (1995) *Conceiving Sexuality. Approaches to Sex Research in a Postmodern World*. New York and London: Routledge.

Petchesky, R. (1987) 'Fetal images: the power of the visual culture in the politics of reproduction', *Feminist Studies*, 13, 2: 263–92.

Petersen, A. and Bunton, R. (eds) (1997) *Foucault, Health and Medicine*. London and New York: Routledge.

Polity (1994) The Polity Reader in Cultural Theory. Cambridge. Polity Press.

Poovey, M. (1989) *Uneven Developments: The Ideological Work of Gender in Mid Victorian England*. London: Virago.

Poovey, M. (1990) 'Speaking of the body: mid-Victorian constructions of female desire', in Jacobus et al. 1990.

Poovey, M. (1992) 'The abortion question and the death of man', in Butler and Scott 1992.

Press Association (1996) 'EU scientists study report in baby milk scare', *Press Association*, 30 May.

Riley, D. (1988) *'Am I That Name?' Feminism and the Category of 'Women' in History*. London: Macmillan Press.

Rose, H. (1983) 'Hand, brain and heart: a feminist epistemology for the natural sciences', *Signs: Journal of Women in Culture and Society*, 9, 1: 73–90.

Rose, H. (1994) *Love, Power and Knowledge*. Cambridge: Polity Press.

Rose, H. and Rose, S. (eds) (1976) *Ideology of/in the Natural Sciences*. Cambridge, MA: Schenkman.

Rose, J. (1986) *Sexuality in the Field of Vision*. London: Verso.

Rowbotham, S. (1977a) *A New World for Women. Stella Browne: Socialist Feminist*. London: Pluto Press.

Rowbotham, S. (1977b) *Hidden from History: 300 Years of Women's Oppression and the Fight Against It*. London: Pluto Press.

Rutherford, J. (1990a) 'A place called home', in Rutherford, 1990b.

Rutherford, J. (ed.) (1990b) *Identity. Community, Culture, Difference*. London: Lawrence and Wishart.

Sawicki, J. (1991) *Disciplining Foucault: Feminism, Power and the Body*. London: Routledge.

Schiebinger, L. (1986) 'Skeletons in the closet: the first illustrations of the female skeleton in nineteenth century anatomy', *Representations*, 14: 42–83.

Schiebinger, L. (1987) 'The history and philosophy of women in science: a review essay', *Signs: Journal of Women in Culture and Society*, 12, 2: 303–32.

Scotsman (1995) 'Fertility under threat' (Leading article), 26 July.

Scotsman (1996) 'Formulaic food scares' (Leading article), *Scotsman*, 28 May.

Scott, J. (1992) 'Experience', in Butler and Scott 1992.

Sears, W. and Little, A. (1996) 'Milking mothers for money', *Northern Echo*, 29 May.

Segal, L. (1994) *Straight Sex: The Politics of Pleasure*. London: Virago.

Seidler, V. (1994) *Unreasonable Men. Masculinity and Social Theory*. London and New York: Routledge.

Sharpe, R. and Skakkebaek, N. (1993) 'Are oestrogens involved in falling sperm counts and disorders of the male reproductive tract?' *Lancet*, 341: 1392–5.

Shuttleworth, S. (1990) 'Female circulation: medical discourse and popular advertising in the mid-Victorian era', in Jacobus et al. 1990.

Smart, C. (1992) 'Disruptive bodies and unruly sex: the regulation of reproduction and sexuality in the nineteenth century', in Smart, C. (ed.). *Regulating Womanhood. Historical Essays on Marriage, Motherhood and Sexuality*. London and New York: Routledge.

Stampfer, M., Colditz, G., Willett, W., Manson, J., Rosner, B., Speizer, F. and Hennekens, C. (1991) 'Postmenopausal estrogen therapy and cardiovascular disease. Ten year follow-up from the Nurses' Health Study', *New England Journal of Medicine*, 325, 11: 756–62.

Stanton, D. C. (ed.) (1992) *Discourses of Sexuality. From Aristotle to AIDS*. Michigan: University of Michigan Press.

Stanworth, M. (ed.) (1987) *Reproductive Technologies : Gender, Motherhood and Medicine*. Cambridge: Polity Press.

Stevenson, N. (1995) *Understanding Media Cultures. Social Theory and Mass Communication*. London, Thousand Oaks and New Delhi: Sage Publications/Open University.

Thompson, J. (1994) 'The theory of the public sphere: a critical appraisal.' In Polity 1994.

Thompson, J. (1995) *The Media and Modernity*. Cambridge: Polity Press.

Thompson, K. (1986) *Beliefs and Ideology*. London and New York: Tavistock Publications.

Thompson, K. (1992) 'Religion, values and ideology', in Bocock, R. and Thompson, K. (eds). *Social and Cultural Forms of Modernity*. Cambridge: Polity Press/Open University.

Tiefer, L. (1995) *Sex Is Not a Natural Act and Other Essays*. Boulder, CO, San Francisco and Oxford: Westview Press.

Treichler, P. (1987) 'AIDS, homophobia and biomedical discourse: an epidemic of signification', *Cultural Studies*, 1, 3: 263–305.

Tuana, N. (ed.) (1989) *Science and Feminism*. Bloomington and Indianapolis: Indiana University Press.

Turner, B. (1984) *The Body and Society*. Oxford: Basil Blackwell.

Turner, B. (1991) 'Recent developments in the theory of the body', in Featherstone, M., Hepworth, M. and Turner, B. (eds). *The Body. Social Process and Cultural Theory*. London: Sage Publications.

Vines, G. (1993) *Raging Hormones. Do They Rule Our Lives?* London: Virago.

Walkowitz, J. (1982) 'Male vice and feminist virtue', *History Workshop Journal*, 13: 175–88.

Weeks, J. (1985) *Sexuality and its Discontents*. London and New York: Routledge.

Weeks, J. (1989) *Sex, Politics and Society. The Regulation of Sexuality since 1800.* London and New York: Longman.

Weeks, J. (1991) *Against Nature: Essays on History, Sexuality and Identity.* London: Rivers Oram Press.

Weeks, J. (1995) 'History, desire, and identities', in Parker and Gagnon 1995.

Wellings, K., Field, J., Johnson, A. M. and Wadsworth, J. (1994) *Sexual Behaviour in Britain. The National Survey of Sexual Attitudes and Lifestyles.* Harmondsworth, Middlesex: Penguin Books.

Williams, R. (1976) *Keywords.* London: Fontana.

Wilson, E. (1990) 'Borderlines', *New Statesman and Society,* 2 (November).

Wilson, R. (1966) *Feminine Forever.* New York: M. Evans.

Wilson, R. A. and Wilson, T. A. (1972) 'The basic philosophy of estrogen maintenance', *Journal of the American Geriatrics Society,* 20: 52–3.

Winston, R. (1993) 'The limits of fertility are being stretched too far in allowing middle-aged women to become mothers', *Guardian,* 21 July.

Wittig, M. (1992a) 'The category of sex', in Wittig 1992c.

Wittig, M. (1992b) 'One is not born a woman', in Wittig 1992c.

Wittig, M. (1992c) *The Straight Mind and Other Essays.* Boston: Beacon Press.

Wood, N. (1985) 'Foucault on the history of sexuality: an introduction', in Beechey, V. and Donald, J. (eds). *Subjectivity and Social Relations.* Milton Keynes: Open University Press.

Woodward, K. (ed.) (1997) *Identity and Difference.* London, Thousand Oaks and New Delhi: Sage Publications/Open University.

Worcester, N. and Whately, M. (1992) 'The selling of HRT: playing on the fear factor', *Feminist Review,* 41: 1–26.

Wren, B. (1992) 'HRT and the cardiovascular system', *Australian Family Physician,* 21, 3: 226–9.

Wright, L. (1996) 'Science and sperm', *Guardian,* 9 March.

Zerilli, L. (1991) 'Rememoration or war? French feminist narrative and the politics of self-representation', *Differences: A Journal of Feminist Cultural Studies,* 3, 1: 1–19.

Zita, J. (1988) 'The pre-menstrual syndrome: "dis-easing" the female cycle', *Hypatia,* 3, 1: 157–68.

Zola, I. K. (1978) 'Medicine as an institution of social control', in Ehrenreich, J. (ed.). *The Cultural Crisis of Modern Medicine.* New York and London: Monthly Review Press.

INDEX